CW00553788

GIRLS IN BLUE

The Story of the Luton Girls Choir

by
Christine Turner

First published September 2001
by
The Book Castle
12 Church Street
Dunstable
Bedfordshire LU5 4RU

ISBN 1 903747 03 1

Typeset & Designed by Priory Graphics, Flitwick, Bedfordshire
Printed by Impress Print, Corby, Northamptonshire

Contents

Acknowledgements

I would like to thank both the many former Choir girls who have shared with me their memories and feelings for the Choir and also those who lent me scrapbooks, photographs and programmes. Thanks to Anne Evans (nee Henry) who shared her thoughts on actually living with Arthur Davies and his wife Gwen and the effect they had on her life.

Thanks also to Malcolm Thatcher and the Luton Library Staff who readily made available Arthur Davies' collection of memorabilia. To the Luton News, Walter Gardiner of Worthing and the BBC for permission to use some of their photographs and to Bob Norman who kindly photographed extra material.

Thank you to Sir James (Jimmy) Saville O.B.E., K.C.S.G., L.L.D., F.C.Y.B., for his memories of the Choir.

Last, but by no means least, a big "Thank You" to Peggy Coggins who pointed me in the right direction, answered thousands of questions and read and re-read the manuscript.

Several other photographs have been used; occasionally I have been unable to trace the photographers for copyright but I have acknowledged them where possible.

Christine Turner

Foreword

Since the Luton Girls Choir disbanded in 1976, I have many times been asked to give talks to various organisations on its history, achievements and how it functioned. As a result it has often been suggested that I should write a book preserving this information, but other commitments made me reluctant to undertake such an arduous task, so I was pleased when, after listening to one of my talks, Christine offered to do this. I was very happy to collaborate with her, using the knowledge I had gained during my long and happy association with this unique Choir.

Thus the story of "Girls in Blue" has come to fruition and I hope it will make enjoyable reading, both for former members to whom it will revive many happy memories and others who found pleasure in seeing and listening to the Choir during its 40 years.

Peggy Coggins
Former Secretary to Arthur E. Davies

ARTHUR E DAVIES M.B.E.
FOUNDER AND MUSICAL DIRECTOR
OF THE LUTON GIRLS CHOIR
1936 – 1976

Chapter One

The Early Years

The Luton Girls Choir spanned 40 years of Luton's growth, making the name of Luton well known both in Britain and around the world. It was an amateur organisation, being a mixture of schoolgirls and young ladies under 24 years old who worked in the local shops, offices and factories. However there was nothing amateurish about their presentation and the girls sang with many famous people, appeared in a film and also sang at the Royal Command Performance.

They toured Australasia and Denmark as well as singing in many British towns. At its peak the Choir was often heard on the radio and seen on television; comedians made jokes about it and it was featured in newspaper cartoons. Other choirs came and went but the Luton Girls Choir survived for 40 years; for its members it was a unique experience and their story deserves a place in history.

The Choir started as a church choir. At 24 years old in 1921 Arthur Davies was appointed as Choir Master of the Wellington Street Baptist Church Choir; with 100 voices it was one of the biggest in Luton and soon became well known, with queues for seats at Sunday School anniversaries and concerts. There would be three anniversary concerts during the Sunday - morning, afternoon and evening - and often instruments would be included. People have described the music as breath taking.

In 1932 the Diaconate asked him to form a special group of 32 voices, from members of the Sunday School, for entry in the first Luton Sunday School Union Eisteddfod. This group included four boys and the choir took first prize in their section, winning the challenge shield. People attended the Church so that their children could join the Junior Choir. In 1933 they won the shield again and when in 1934 they won for a third time, according to the rules, the shield went to the choir which came second and they received a special Diploma. In 1935 the Choir went further afield and won the Challenge Cup first prize at the Balham and Streatham Music Festival.

In 1936 the Ceylon Baptist Junior Choir was auditioned by "Uncle Mac" for a possible radio appearance. They actually broadcast on London Regional BBC's Children's Hour on two occasions, October 16th and December 20th. At this time Mr Davies found the test transmission more worrying than the actual broadcast which he was allowed to conduct in his shirt sleeves. It was found that the Choir followed his movements so closely it was only necessary to place the microphone a few inches from his elbow to get the best sound. The October programme consisted of general songs, the one in December of carols, with some of the girls singing solos. These broadcasts were a sensational achievement for the Choir

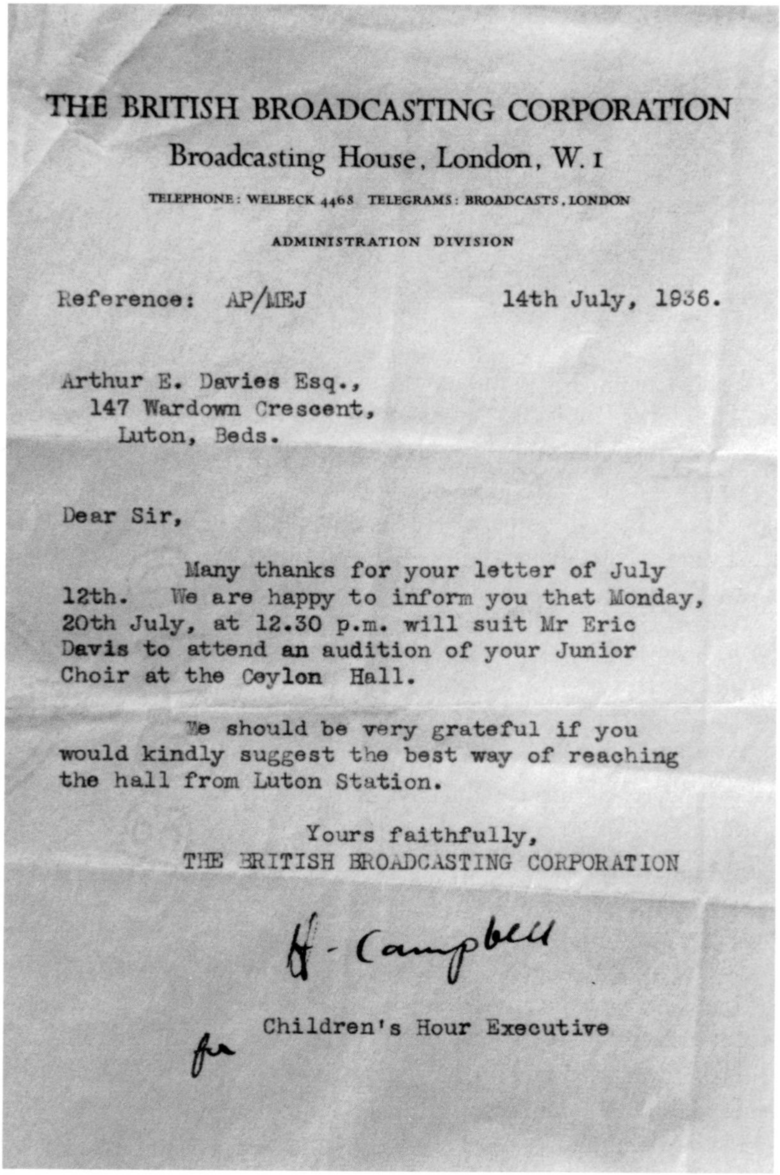

THE BRITISH BROADCASTING CORPORATION
Broadcasting House, London, W. 1
TELEPHONE: WELBECK 4468 TELEGRAMS: BROADCASTS, LONDON
ADMINISTRATION DIVISION

Reference: AP/MEJ 14th July, 1936.

Arthur E. Davies Esq.,
147 Wardown Crescent,
Luton, Beds.

Dear Sir,

Many thanks for your letter of July 12th. We are happy to inform you that Monday, 20th July, at 12.30 p.m. will suit Mr Eric Davis to attend an audition of your Junior Choir at the Ceylon Hall.

We should be very grateful if you would kindly suggest the best way of reaching the hall from Luton Station.

Yours faithfully,
THE BRITISH BROADCASTING CORPORATION

H. Campbell

for Children's Hour Executive

Letter from the BBC in preparation for the first broadcast. Photo Bob Norman.

and for the next few years the letters BBC followed their name on all programmes and announcements.

Grace Crew can remember the first broadcast very clearly. Aged 12 years old, she was allowed to have the day off school and go with the Choir to Broadcasting House in Portland Place. Although they could not be seen, the girls all had to wear their Choir dresses and Grace had a new pair of shoes for the occasion. Unfortunately the shoes "squeaked". During the rehearsal "Uncle Mac" came over

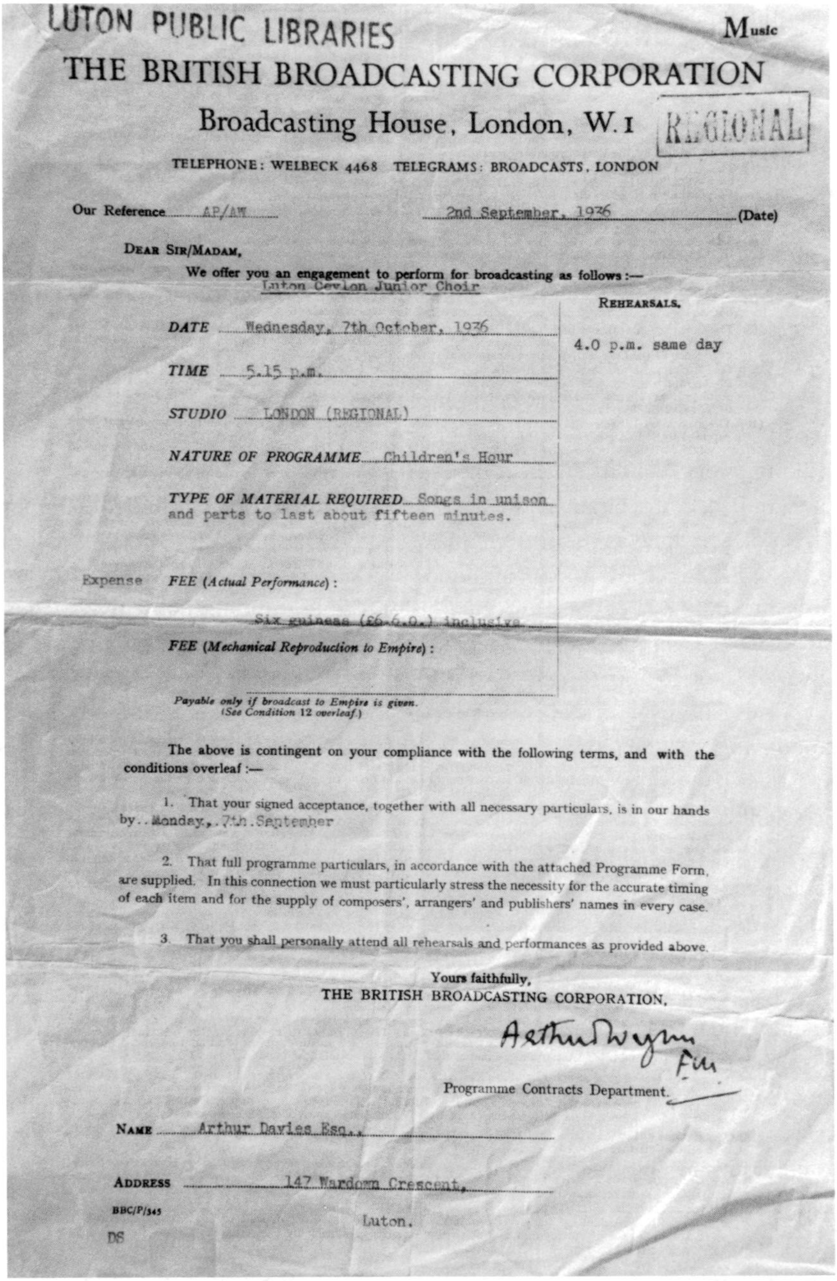

Music

THE BRITISH BROADCASTING CORPORATION

Broadcasting House, London, W.1 REGIONAL

TELEPHONE: WELBECK 4468 TELEGRAMS: BROADCASTS, LONDON

Our Reference AP/AW 2nd September, 1936 (Date)

DEAR SIR/MADAM,

We offer you an engagement to perform for broadcasting as follows:—
Luton Ceylon Junior Choir

DATE Wednesday, 7th October, 1936

TIME 5.15 p.m.

STUDIO LONDON (REGIONAL)

NATURE OF PROGRAMME Children's Hour

TYPE OF MATERIAL REQUIRED Songs in unison and parts to last about fifteen minutes.

REHEARSALS. 4.0 p.m. same day

Expense FEE (Actual Performance):

Six guineas (£6.6.0.) inclusive

FEE (Mechanical Reproduction to Empire):

Payable only if broadcast to Empire is given.
(See Condition 12 overleaf.)

The above is contingent on your compliance with the following terms, and with the conditions overleaf:—

1. That your signed acceptance, together with all necessary particulars, is in our hands by.. Monday,. 7th. September

2. That full programme particulars, in accordance with the attached Programme Form, are supplied. In this connection we must particularly stress the necessity for the accurate timing of each item and for the supply of composers', arrangers' and publishers' names in every case.

3. That you shall personally attend all rehearsals and performances as provided above.

Yours faithfully,
THE BRITISH BROADCASTING CORPORATION.
Arthur Wynn
Programme Contracts Department.

NAME Arthur Davies Esq.,

ADDRESS 147 Wardown Crescent,
Luton.

BBC/P/345

DS

Payment Record from the BBC for the first broadcast. Photo Bob Norman

to speak to her. He admired her shoes very much but had to ask her if she would mind taking them off for the broadcast, as the "squeak" would be heard during the programme. Grace describes Uncle Mac as "so lovely that the girls were virtually eating out of his hand". Of course she did not mind taking off her shoes and singing in her socks. Other stars on Children's Hour were "Uncle David", David Davies, and "Aunt Elizabeth", Elizabeth Jenkins, both being extremely pleasant to work with. As Grace was already a fan of "Children's Hour" she found the whole session unbelievably thrilling. This was compounded the next day when she was asked at the school assembly to tell the whole school about her experiences.

Mr Davies was spending more time with just the junior choir than was appreciated by the church dignitaries and in the end it was decided that he would leave the Ceylon Baptist Church and form his own girls choir. This meant that the boys who were also members of the choir were no longer able to sing with the girls. At the request of the Mayor of Luton it was called The Luton Girls Choir and was then open to any girl in the area. Although those joining from the Ceylon Baptist Church were expected to remain members of the Sunday School, Grace said it initially only felt as if the Choir had changed rehearsal rooms as the Junior Choir did not sing every Sunday in the Church, only on special occasions.

The Choir became larger and could then add 2 and 4 part songs to its repertoire, their first performance as the Luton Girls Choir taking place in Bury Park Memorial Hall in November 1936 to an audience of 230 people. Initially the Choir had difficulty in finding a rehearsal room and for a time it met at the Hawkes's home in Cromwell Road, Margaret Hawkes becoming its first secretary. When more funds were available the Choir moved to the Railway Mission in Station Road. Over the years various rooms and halls were used for rehearsals including the old Corn Exchange and later the Connaught Hall in Upper George Street above Day's music shop. There was also a NAAFI Club at the rear of the Electricity showrooms where the girls would arrive on the Sunday morning to find the air thick with cigarette smoke and the stale smell of beer from the previous evening's club meeting. They did not consider the dangers to the voice from passive smoking in those days. Eventually the Choir was registered as a youth club and could use rooms at Youth Headquarters. These were first at the old hat factory warehouse on the corner of Bridge Street and Guildford Street and later in Waller Street. When the latter was demolished, the Choir moved to Langley Street School, then to Queen's Square and finally to Surrey Street.

Mr Davies was still as keen to win competitions and he expected a very high standard from each girl. He demanded attendance at every rehearsal come what may. One member's mother asked if her daughter could be excused because she had a boil in her ear. The answer was "no" and she had to attend the practice.

There were concerts every week, sometimes twice a week and songs would be rehearsed until Mr Davies was satisfied. They would go over a number again and again until it came together and the girls can remember going home after a concert feeling exhilarated and still singing.

During the early 30's when the Choir performed, there was an advert on the programme saying Mr Davies gave singing and choral conducting lessons at the studio of S. Farmer and Co.

In March 1938 the Choir entered the London Music Festival at Westminster, having to compete generally as they were no longer a Sunday School Choir. They won first place in the senior section for Girls Clubs and Friendly Societies, the first time the thirty girls from 9 to 17 years old had entered a senior competition. The test pieces were "Piper's Song" by Rutland Boughton, for which the Choir gained 85 marks and "An Eriskay Love Lilt" arranged by M. Kennedy Fraser which earned them 88 marks. Three girls, Edna Kaye, Bessie Walker and Diana Raggatt also won places in the individual classes. In April the Choir and the three girls then had to sing in a prize winners concert at the Central Hall Westminster.

During the first few years of the Choir the programme would contain poetry readings as well as the songs. Some of the poems would be written by the girls themselves; one such was Peggy Adams who wrote "England". At a concert in November 1938 there were four poetry readings, six soloists and 36 girls singing.

Even in those days Mr Davies knew what he wanted and a note at the bottom of one concert programme read, "This programme is timed for exactly two hours, so your applause may be strong but not too long".

One of the Choir's aims was to raise money for charity and at the concert in 1938 in Bury Park Memorial Hall, nurses from the Bute Hospital made a silver collection for the Mayor's "New Hospital Appeal". By April 1939 the programme notes state that the Choir had given 200 concerts and raised about £800 for charities and chapel appeals. In December the total was £1000 and the Choir celebrated, wearing white dresses with blue trimmings at their next concert in Chapel Street Methodist Church Hall.

Their singing always won the competitions and in the 1939 Grand Challenge Shield at the London Music Festival the Choir again won their class. So did one of their soloists, 10 year old Maureen Hough, gaining a distinction for her singing of "Shirley Temple" songs. Mr Davies heard her sing when she was only 7 years old but her mother would not let her join the Choir until she was 9. She sang as a soloist for 3 years before tragically dying at the age of 12 in 1941. Again, after three straight wins the Choir could no longer enter this competition.

Mr Davies began to think that the spirit of rivalry and competition might soon come before the girls' love of singing for its own sake and he stopped entering competitions and concentrated on bringing music to the greatest possible number of people.

By the end of the 1930's the Choir was also becoming well known in the surrounding towns and villages. There was little other entertainment except the cinema and wireless and the Choir was very popular. They often performed in churches, with the girls perched rather perilously on chairs and choir stalls. One girl remembers having to sing like an angel while condensation dripped from the window down her neck. Another time the hall was locked at Wolverton when the

Choir arrived. The caretaker eventually appeared and unlocked the door but there was no piano. Undeterred, Mr Davies borrowed one from a neighbouring house and press ganged two people passing by to help him move it into the hall. The show must go on. The girls had to make their own way to the concert venue and back again afterwards, often travelling by train to Flitwick and Bedford. At the latter they would give two concerts for the Salvation Army, one in the afternoon and one in the evening. In between shows the Choir were invited home to tea by members of the congregation.

The early years, about 1939. Photo Luton News.

The Choir, 1940. Photo Luton News.

When war was declared in 1939 there were initial fears about the difficulties of transport and the blackout. After a while the Government changed its mind about people gathering together and encouraged all sorts of entertainment to keep up people's morale. During this time the Choir played a vital part in the war effort, providing good entertainment and raising thousands of pounds for war charities such as service men's comfort funds and money for refugees from occupied countries. There were "Digging for Victory" and "Warship Weeks", "National Savings Drives" and many similar national appeals.

The Choir's main service was probably raising the spirits of thousands of folk during the time of restrictions, rationing, shortages and queues. They were popular with the troops and sang for them in various venues. Grace Goring ran a canteen for the military at the Corn Exchange and the Choir also sang there on a regular basis, always to a full house.

The blackout restrictions caused the Choir to change their rehearsals from Friday night to Sunday morning but they still travelled up to London during the week for recording sessions. After evening concerts the girls would walk home in a group, singing in the dark.

In May 1940 the Choir numbered 38 but when they started to sing in the larger halls and cinemas more voices were needed, so the number rose to 50. The first concerts in the Odeon and Union cinemas were a thrilling experience for the girls and in 1941 they were paid £10 for a performance at the Union Cinema. The setting was quite different to the churches and halls which they had been used to and of course the darkness, necessary for films, made it impossible to see the audience beyond the first row. One former member describes the audience as being under a cloud of black velvet.

The spotlights were on the Choir, stepping out onto the staging; they were told to be relaxed but with no slouching. "Think of how you look from the front, girls" was the command. They had to rehearse in situ before a cinema performance as the acoustics were quite different to those of a concert hall, not so sharp, almost woolly. Given a chord to sing and with alternated breathing they kept the chord while Mr Davies wandered all round the stalls making sure even the pianissimo singing could be heard adequately.

There was always a well known guest artiste and Ronnie Waldman was usually the compere. Henry Cummings was one of the favourites, so friendly and willing to joke and laugh with the girls during the interval. Eileen Joyce with her change of dress for the second half and John McCormack, the Irish Tenor, also appeared. It was the pianists Rawicz and Landauer who provided Grace Crew with one of her funny memories. On one occasion the Choir were about to start the second half when the girl who stood next to her was missing. Seconds before the curtain was drawn back she puffed into place looking extremely red and giggling. "I went to Rawicz and Landauer's dressing room to get their autograph" she said. "I knocked and thought they said "Come in" so I did and they were in their underpants". What they had said was "We're changing" but their Austrian accent got in the way. Both girls found the second half difficult to get through, especially when the guest artists appeared. It was when the Choir started to sing at the larger venues that they began to appear with regimental and military bands. These sounded better than brass bands in the larger halls and this later became quite a feature of their concerts.

The Choir were heard several times on the wireless in 1942. On the 12th of February a concert for "Warship Week" was broadcast from Dunstable. The venue was not specified, it was listed in the Radio Times as a "Join in and Sing" programme with "Leslie Woodgate conducting a civilian audience in national and popular songs. Henry Cummings leads the singing and the Luton Girls Choir with their conductor Arthur Davies contribute to the programme". The broadcast was only for half an hour but the concert in Dunstable went on for longer.

In April they appeared again on Children's Hour with Uncle Mac, one member being fascinated by the flimsy paper used for his script to prevent rustling noises as the pages were turned. Also in April the Choir took part in the BBC's "Britain Sings" series, being heard on four different services, North America, the Pacific, the African and the Eastern service. They were still singing at concerts in the local cinemas and they appeared with Rawicz and Landauer and Roy Henderson at the Alma Theatre in July.

During the summer months the Home Entertainment Committee arranged "Holiday at Home" concerts for the workers and the Choir was the main attraction. At these concerts in Wardown Park, Uncle Arthur and John Gibbs (from the Luton News) organised talent competitions. One young girl won three times running and Mr Davies was so impressed that he asked her mother if the youngster, Patricia Corley, could join the Luton Girls Choir. She went on to play a prominent part in the Choir activities for many years.

Concerts still included poetry and Zena Rocliffe was asked to write short poems lasting about 3 to 4 minutes which she then read during the performance. Her first was "Their Finest Hour" written at the beginning of the war and for "War Weapons Week" she wrote "Cry of Silence". The rest of the girls listened to these poems many times and one can still quote the words even today.

The Choir were still travelling to the villages and a note on the programme for a concert at Hitchin in November said the performance was at the weekend as transport difficulties curtailed a mid week visit. Travelling during the war was not easy and whenever possible the Choir went by train; petrol was rationed and they could only travel so many miles by coach.

There was a hitch in the arrangements when in September 1943 Mr Davies thought he would try taking the Choir to the larger neighbouring town of Watford, to perform at the Town hall. The Choir appeared with the Beds and Herts

Regimental Band, the proceeds going to their prisoner of war fund. Some members of the Choir actually lived in Dunstable and Mr Davies announced during the programme that these girls had walked over to Luton in the morning as no buses had been running. This sort of dedication became the hallmark of the girls throughout the life of the Choir. He also made an appeal for pennies and half pennies for Choir funds and £14 was raised.

All was well until the return journey. The Choir had travelled to St Albans by train and then by coach on to Watford. After the concert the girls boarded the two coaches and duly arrived back at St Albans. Peggy Hawkes was in charge of one coach and Grace Crew the other. They all assembled outside the station and found, as Grace put it, "We had left the boss and his wife behind". Both had thought Mr and Mrs Davies were in the other coach. What did they do? There was no public transport from Watford at 10.30pm at night. During much biting of nails and worrying, a little army van appeared in the station yard; surreptitiously the back was opened and literally out rolled Mr and Mrs Davies! Army vehicles were not supposed to carry unofficial civilians so the passengers had been concealed in transit and quickly tipped out on arrival. Fortunately, once they were all reunited, the guilty parties were forgiven but not allowed to forget for a long while afterwards. This trip was actually the first of many visits to Watford in the Choir's long history.

Regular appearances at Luton's cinemas continued during 1943. In November a concert with the band of the Royal Air Force Bomber Command raised money for the "British Sailor's Society", while a rather unusual charity benefited from their two concerts on the 21st November when they appeared with the Vauxhall Motors' Concert Orchestra and a group called the "Revellers Entertainers". This was the Luton Borough Police Boot Fund for Poor Children. During the proceeding eight years 4,000 pairs of boots had been provided at a cost of £2,000.

In the last full year of war the Choir sang on another visit to Watford with the Beds and Herts Regiment in January and a note in the programme said "girls have this last seven days given up three evenings to music, in addition to normal rehearsing, for this concert due to the influenza epidemic".

At a "Salute the Soldier" savings rally the front of the programme was decorated with a picture of a bug and bore the words "Stamp on the Squander Bug." Luton had adopted some air force squadrons and during the evening there was an exchange of log books and a plaque between Wing Commander Christopher Currant and the Mayor.

A Sunday concert in Welwyn Garden City provided more worry for Grace Crew, amusing to look back on but upsetting at the time. The only way to get to Welwyn by train from Luton was on the LMS line to St Albans, then a walk up a hill for quite a way to a small station on the LNER line to Welwyn. The Choir were accompanied by a local cellist, Eileen Croxford. She later became well known in the musical world but at that time she was just making her way and Mr Davies, having heard her play, asked her to appear with the Choir at some of their concerts. Eileen viewed the walk between stations with dismay, saying that if she had to carry her cello all the time it would strain her bow arm and she would not be able to play so well. Grace and her friend offered to carry this awkward instrument and, not being used to hauling such a load around, made rather heavy weather of the job. It was a hot day and they reached the station with some relief, only to find that they had lagged so far behind the rest of the girls, that the train with the rest of the Choir aboard was just leaving the station.

Struggling down two flights of stairs in a panic they were met by the station master who asked them where they were going. They explained their predicament and he said "Never mind, leave it to me". A few minutes later he reappeared from his office and told them he had arranged for the next train through the station to stop and pick them up. What a relief. What he had not told them was that the train was a troop train full of soldiers. Grace can still remember today the fun those soldiers had with such remarks as "You can sit on my lap ducks but not with that thing" and "Hey love, do you ride it side saddle?" By the time they arrived the two girls were in a helpless state of giggles and struggled off the train at Welwyn amid lots of cat calls. As Grace said "At least we made a carriage full of troops happy".

Another uphill walk greeted the two girls but they were met part way by a group from the Choir, Mr and Mrs Davies and a tearful Eileen Croxford, the latter convinced she would never see her cello again. Everybody was pleased to see the player and instrument reunited, Grace felt nobody was unduly worried about them and worse still the lunch which had been provided for the Choir had all been eaten. They enjoyed telling the others about having the troop train stopped especially for them, but vowed never to offer to carry anything heavier than a piccolo in future.

The war time concerts always finished in a patriotic fashion. The Choir would sing "There'll Always be an England" and on the last line each girl would unfurl and wave a small flag.

Chapter Two

Joining and Singing in the Choir

The Choir was only open to girls living within a 5 mile radius of Luton and most of them approached Mr Davies with a request to join; there were only a few that he actually asked himself, having heard them sing elsewhere. Each potential member would be asked to attend an audition before the general Choir rehearsal, and sing a song of her own choice. One member described her audition as a singing lesson, with Arthur Davies singing to illustrate breathing techniques and working hard to get the best from her. The girls were judged on their choice of song, sense of pitch and voice control.

Singing was only part of the test, psychology also played a large part in the audition. Mr Davies spent time talking to the prospective member to see if she was "hard" or "mouldable". He wanted girls that would heed discipline without resentment, who would be loyal, sincere and adhere to the Christian principles of life. The girl must be modest, able to conduct herself properly in public and to sing for the sheer joy of it. Team spirit was essential; if a girl was found to be self centred and wanted to get on at the expense of the Choir she was dropped.

The girls were expected to put the Choir first before anything else, including family and friends. He would read out the list of singers for the weekend on the Friday evening and the Choir would depart at lunch time on the Saturday. This made personal arrangements very difficult.

He was nearly always right in his choice. Girls would sometimes leave for various reasons, such as pressure from school work, boyfriends or the fact that there was little free time. However, for those who stayed with him over the years, the feeling was two way; he cared for his girls and they would do anything for him. He often said that success in running the Choir was due to 40% psychology and 60% singing. During the first years of the Choir's life if the girl was successful at her audition she attended rehearsals only, until her dress was ready. This was made at Alexander's in Wellington Street. She would then be able to sing with the Choir. In later years the applicant would receive a letter of acceptance and would be on probation for six months. There were generally about 12 - 15 probationers and after their training would come another test; this passed, the girl could then join the main Choir. Retirement from the Choir was before the 24th birthday or upon marriage, Mr Davies maintaining that it was a "girls" choir and also a wife's duty was to her husband.

When the Choir became established, parents were asked to complete a questionnaire on behalf of the applicant; it almost amounted to a contract. Apart from pertinent questions about the girl's health and ability to travel by coach or rail, the parent had to agree that the girl would attend two rehearsals a week as well as be available for concerts. They were also asked to maintain the Choir uniform. Mr Davies needed assurance that the girl was aware of the self sacrifice that membership of the Choir would involve and that she was of even temper, helpful and co-operative in every respect. They also had to promise that a six month notice of retirement would be given to cover "risks both financial and artistic, associated with future planning of this voluntary organisation".

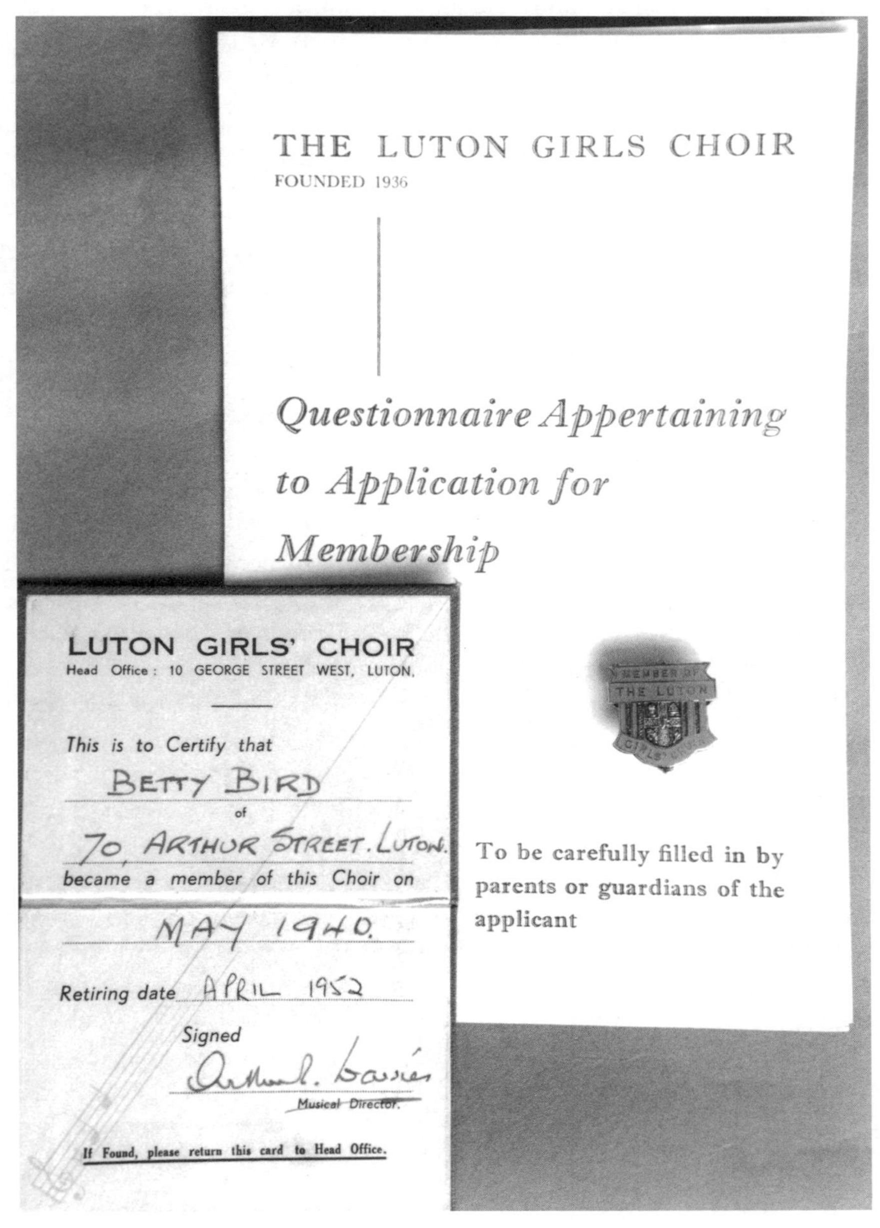
THE LUTON GIRLS CHOIR
FOUNDED 1936

Questionnaire Appertaining to Application for Membership

To be carefully filled in by parents or guardians of the applicant

LUTON GIRLS' CHOIR
Head Office: 10 GEORGE STREET WEST, LUTON.

This is to Certify that
BETTY BIRD
of
70, ARTHUR STREET. LUTON.
became a member of this Choir on
MAY 1940.

Retiring date APRIL 1952

Signed
Arthur J. Davies
Musical Director.

If Found, please return this card to Head Office.

Application form, membership card and Choir badge. Photo Bob Norman.

The Choir started with about 45 girls but by 1949, with larger venues and the need for more volume and tone, the numbers had gradually risen, first to 60 then 65 then to 70 girls singing at concerts, recording sessions and broadcasts. In the 1950's about 2 out of every 30 applicants were successful. By the mid '60s when the coaches became larger it was often uneconomical to run two and to feed so many girls, so the number for concerts was reduced to 56.

In a copy of the "Bedfordshire Topic" for 1966 it reported the number of girls in the Choir as 85, 20 on probation and those singing at concerts as between 45 - 75 depending on venue. A "pool" of girls was needed, as Mr Davies was expected to supply the number of girls stated in the contract and there would always be some who could not attend.

On acceptance to the Choir the girls received a letter which included the words "You will need to practice the art of becoming a first class citizen and an ambassador for the town you represent, especially when a guest in other people's homes in towns you may never before have visited". Some recipients of this letter were school girls of only 12 or 13 years old but were expected to adhere to the same high standards.

The girl was given the coveted gold and blue Luton Girls Choir badge and their name was engraved on the back. They also received their membership card giving the date on which they joined the Choir, the leaving date being added at the appropriate time. Each girl paid a subscription; at first this was 4d a week, increasing to 1/- and finally 25p. In the 50's girls would be earning about 15/- a week. These subs helped towards the cost of rehearsal rooms and general expenses.

The Choir was eventually affected by the performance laws which stated that children under 15 must be licensed, could not appear professionally on the stage on Sundays and must leave any stage by 10pm. This obviously governed where the younger ones could sing and members can remember having to leave the stage and sit in the coach at some concerts. It also made Mr Davies's job of selection and balance more difficult. Younger members did not go to coastal venues such as Eastbourne or Folkestone as these concerts would be on a Sunday, in theatres and finish later. They could only appear commercially 12 times a year and had to be chaperoned away from home.

Mr Davies organised periodic voice tests when he would hear each girl sing separately. He would then advise them and sort out "timbre" or woolly resonance. He would put the girls in groups varying from duets to octets and would pick out future soloists; he would also sometimes move girls from the sopranos to the mezo sopranos.

Mr Davies did not believe in formal singing lessons for the younger girls but several of the over 16's had lessons with a Madame Groombridge who lived in Russell Rise. She was a well endowed lady given to wearing black chenille and chiffon. Timing would be tapped out with a knitting needle kept on the piano and the girls were also given lessons in deportment, large books being balanced on the head while walking up and down stairs. The same books were placed on the diaphragm while the girl was lying on the floor; the books had to rise with the breathing. The girls remember with amusement the collection of rubber rain shoes, fishermen's rubber hats and brollys all kept in the hall and handed out to the girls to use if it was raining when they went home.

A rehearsal in the late 1940's. Photo Luton News.

At concerts new soloists were gradually introduced; the programme would read "a new voice", no name would be given. When the girl was established, her name would then appear opposite the song. Individual encores were not allowed, Mr Davies felt that everybody worked equally hard and there would be no favourites and no jealousy.

The girls did not sing from music, each song being learnt by heart before a performance. Sometimes it could take 8½ hours of practice for a 4 minute number but once learnt it would be retained by the Choir. Sometimes Mr Davies would give a word picture to try to explain a meaning behind one of the songs. Rehearsals were always demanding and the songs would be practised until perfect. In spite of the hard work, girls can remember finishing on a "high". They would still be singing as they walked home through the streets. There would also be separate rehearsals for the different groups, i.e sopranos, mezzos and contraltos, while the soloists often practised individually at Mr Davies's home.

Most of the music was arranged especially for the Choir and this helped to give it that unique sound. At first Mr Davies did the arranging but later it was done by other people. At one time they needed an arrangement of "Silent Night" very quickly. George Melachrino just sat and wrote it in his London office while Mr Davies waited, then Mr Davies dashed to St Pancras by taxi to catch the train back to Luton in time for a rehearsal that same evening.

Over the years Mr Davies introduced new ideas into the repertoire. In 1955/6 there was the "echo" gimmick where a small group would go into the gallery or to the other end of the room and sing an echo to the version being sung by the body of the Choir. At one time he was accused of cruelty as one of his tricks was to hold the girls on the last note of a song, then turn to the audience and introduce the next item while the girls held the note. This trick received great applause at the Festival Hall in 1952 but some people said this was cruel and would damage the girl's lungs. The girls were not worried, as they were trained to breathe and sing.

In 1964 he devised his own way to round off the square vowels which were part of the Bedfordshire accent. This helped the words to be heard more clearly.

There were always some songs which were greater favourites with the girls than others but all had to be sung to perfection. To start a concert Mr Davies would click his fingers and the girls would immediately lift their hands up in front of their waists and be ready. This action fascinated the audience as they did not hear the click and were amazed at the precision of the movement. There were some critics who felt this was rather contrived but to the girls it seemed a natural place for the hands.

All the girls had to be able to see Mr Davies as he directed them from the piano with his facial expressions, mouthing the words as they were sung. Each girl had to keep her eyes fixed on his face for instruction. He would know if any girl was not watching him and tell her he had noticed at the next rehearsal.

Over the years this method of control also fascinated many people. While the Choir were in Aberystwyth for the final concert of the Mid Wales Eisteddfod, two of the adjudicators were overheard to remark that they were going to stay on after the competition and listen to this Luton Girls Choir. They understood Mr Davies did not conduct the girls in the orthodox manner but just directed them from the piano. This contradicted all they had been preaching to the competing choirs, i.e that a good down beat by the conductor was essential.

In an article on the Choir in "John Bull" in 1952 it said "the Choir's formula of music was "Music you Know and Love". Most of the songs are "old masters" - first class ballads of yesterday and present day ballads with good lines, supplemented by items from opera, operetta, musical comedy and films. The words should preferably be sacred, sentimental or philosophical and appropriate for young girls". This successful formula was used throughout the Choir's existence.

Senior girls were chosen to introduce the evening while others said "Good night" at the end of the concert. At first Mr Davies would write their script but after a while he would give them a copy of the programme and leave the choice of words to the commere. The girls would be introduced to their role by being given the job of saying "Thank you" for the hospitality shown to the Choir while on their week end tours. They would generally have tea or lunch en route and a prospective commere would get her first taste of public speaking to a reasonably small group.

When the time came for a girl to leave the Choir she could choose her last concert venue and she would be presented with an eight day clock. There are many cherished clocks around the country.

One of the "Retirement Clocks". Photo Bob Norman.

Chapter Three

Further from Home

At last the war ended and at the cessation of hostilities in 1945 Mr Davies thought he would like to take his Choir much further afield on a singing holiday. With this in mind the Choir gave a Summer Serenade concert at the Luton Odeon in June to raise funds for the trip. Pianos were loaned for the occasion by Farmers who also advertised the concert in their shop windows in Wellington Street. During the concert the Luton Band played a piece called "A Fanfare to Victory" especially composed for the event by E.S Carter and, at 10 years old, Patricia Corley, wearing her pyjamas and a dressing gown, made her debut as a soloist singing "Christopher Robin is Saying his Prayers". At the end of the first half the deputy Mayor, Alderman John Burgoyne, paid tribute to the work of the Choir, saying that by 1944 they had raised £6,000 for war charities.

August was the month set for the holiday and the west coast was the area. No concert agent was interested in arranging the tour due to problems of transport and accommodation. Through a colleague of Mr Sidney Farmer, contacts were made in Weston Super Mare. The Rank Organisation gave permission for the 2,600 seater Odeon cinema to rearrange its programme and allow the Choir to give a concert after the first house on Sunday night 19th August. Ronnie Waldman was the compere and the concert was in aid of a local hospital. All the tickets were sold and more than 500 people were turned away. These were later accommodated at concerts in a local Methodist church.

On Monday the Choir gave a concert at the Victoria Rooms in Bristol. The programme was broadcast and the compere was again Ronnie Waldman. Marie Robinson felt that it was Ronnie Waldman's appreciation of the Choir which led to them getting so many broadcasts and recording sessions. At a second concert on Wednesday in the Central Hall Bristol the first half of the programme was again broadcast. On Thursday the girls were back in Weston Super Mare at the Victoria Methodist Church. According to the programme this was a "Choral Thanksgiving with the Choir in a more cultural vein". It seemed that the people of Weston Super Mare appreciated the Choir's singing more than the people of Bristol and an extra concert was arranged at the church on the Friday evening to accommodate those people still wanting to hear them sing. In Weston they sang to overflowing halls while in Bristol the audience was rather sparse.

These were still days of rationing and when going away for a week, ration books had to be taken or an emergency card obtained; provisions were made for guests in hotels. While the girls were in Weston Super Mare, 30 - 35 of them stayed at the Blue Triangle Club house, the rest being accommodated in private houses. Four chaperones travelled with the Choir and the services of a doctor and nurse were on hand if needed.

Zena Rocliffe had not seen the sea since before the war and on her first morning she walked a long way out on the beach for a paddle. She did not find the sea but soon found she was up to her knees in sand. The girls spent their free mornings on the beach but it was not until the night of the last concert, when they were returning home, that they actually saw the sea up to the promenade. This was Zena's last appearance with the Choir as a member and although she was leaving to get married she was very upset to go, an experience shared over the years by many of the girls. Several talk of being moved to tears when they hear records of the Choir which bring back so many good memories.

On January 22nd 1946 two coach loads of friends and family went to His Majesty's Theatre in London to listen to their Choir recording a radio programme called "The Big Event". This was later broadcast to soldiers on the overseas network on the 23rd January and on the Light programme on February 13th. 55 girls spent the whole day in London in the company of many of the best known West End stage and radio stars including Nervo and Knox, Maudie Evans, Richard Murdoch and Kenneth Horne. The morning was spent rehearsing, followed by lunch at one of the BBC canteens and the recording was done in the afternoon. They sang three songs, "Tales from the Vienna Woods", "Greensleeves", and "We'll Gather Lilacs" and then joined Stanley Black and the Dance Orchestra in the finale - Ronnie Waldman was again the compere. The girls then had tea in a Coventry Street restaurant before returning home.

Although the Choir were making regular broadcasts and were appearing in shows with established names, some professional entertainers were initially doubtful about appearing with a "collection of schoolgirls". The no nonsense, disciplined approach of Mr Davies always won them over. When they were asked to accompany Richard Tauber in a series of programmes, however, he refused to sing with a "bunch of amateurs". At the peak of his fame, he demanded the highest possible standards. The broadcasts were being organised by Ronnie Waldman and he took Richard Tauber to the studios where the girls were rehearsing, singing Landon Ronald's "Oh Lovely Night". Tauber listened motionless and transfixed for five minutes before thrusting open the doors and bursting into the studio. There were tears streaming down his face as he congratulated the girls on their singing. From then on they were good friends and the proceeds of one of the Choir's first recordings went to the Richard Tauber Memorial Scholarship.

On May 13th 1946 Richard Tauber was given the "Freedom of the Air" during the radio programme "Monday Night at Eight". It was part of the show called "The Monday Birthday Party" and featured a well known person celebrating his anniversary and being given several wishes, the host of the show during 1946/7 being Kenneth Horne.

Tauber wanted to hear the sounds of Broadway so that he could get used to them before his forthcoming visit to America, to sing "You are my Hearts Delight" in three languages, to hear the voice of one of his Hollywood friends and to listen to the Luton Girls Choir sing one of his songs. They had recently appeared with him in his Christmas show.

The Choir were assembled at Luton Grammar School, connected by BBC engineers to the studio. 50 - 60 voices wished him "Happy Birthday" and sang for him "My Heart and I". The girls only knew about the evening less than a fortnight before the broadcast and hurried rehearsals had to take place. Mr Davies had returned early to Luton from his holiday especially for the event. Richard Tauber thought the BBC had failed on his last request and asked anxiously "Where are they?" but all was well.

In the April of 1946 the Choir sang at Harpenden in the same programme as Tommy Handley, who said that one of the things which had made him agree to appear was the fact that the Luton Girls Choir was singing too. The girls found him friendly and full of fun. One member who could not stand listening to ITMA was not too keen on being on the same programme as Mr Handley but even she was won over by his warm and ebullient character.

He also appeared on the "Freedom of the Air" on January 13th 1947 and one of his wishes was that the Choir should sing "We'll Gather Lilacs" for him. The show was again hosted by Kenneth Horne and the girls were in Luton. He said "Are you there Mr Davies?" The reply, " Yes, and there is a member of the Choir who wishes to say a word or two to Tommy Handley. She is Sheila Potter aged 14 years". Sheila, "Is Mr Handley there?" Tommy Handley, "Yes I'm here dear". Sheila, "Well here's wishing you Many Happy Returns and everybody in the Choir says the same. We send this music to you with affectionate birthday wishes". Tommy Handley, "Well that's real nice". Tommy Handley said he had chosen the Choir after hearing them sing for Richard Tauber.

Yvonne James remembers the day as she was really too young to sing on the radio but Mr Davies said she had worked so hard she could go on, as long as she kept a low profile.

Touring

Word got round after the Weston Super Mare tour that this chap Davies had a good Choir and they were willing to travel. This in turn brought increasing organisational problems as he then had to consider transport, halls, programmes and publicity in distant towns, as well as accommodation for the girls.

The National Children's Home took up the idea of sponsoring the Choir tours and as the Homes were supported by the Methodists, members of the congregations were persuaded to provide free overnight bed and board for the girls. The concert would be the focal point of the "Sunny Smiles" collections and these would be presented at the end of the performance. Each concert would have a local eminent chairperson who sent out invitations to wealthy people in the area. The NCH would fund the hire of the halls and transport costs and would keep the ticket money from the concerts; there would be a collection for the Choir during the interval. Thus in 1945 the pattern was set for many years of weekend tours all over Britain. Many of the programmes for the concerts were printed at the Printing Technical School of the NCH in Harpenden and later they also included a leaflet advertising a "League of Light Lantern" for tuppence halfpenny per week - the price of a postage stamp.

During the summer the Choir would sing at the coast and in the winter they would go inland; the venues would be close together like Bournemouth and Southampton, Leicester and Rugby. The seaside concerts were not sponsored by the Children's Home but were organised by the resorts entertainments managers as Sunday night "Celebrity Concerts" in the towns of Eastbourne, Worthing, Folkestone and Margate; the Choir sometimes appeared with other artistes, sometimes on their own. At Bank Holidays the tour would be longer, with the Choir often going on the Friday and returning to Luton on the Monday night; these tours could be further afield in Cornwall, Wales or Blackpool. On the occasions when the Choir members were not billeted with local people there could be a problem with accommodation, especially at peak holiday time. In 1951 while singing at Bournemouth some of the girls actually had to stay in Salisbury.

A regular pattern emerged and the Choir would appear at the same venues at approximately the same time each year. There was always a concert at Watford, sometimes two a year, and there would be Sunday concerts for various London Boroughs. In Luton the Choir gradually restricted its singing and later only performed there three or four times a year.

A typical weekend would start at Saturday lunch time, as many of the girls worked in the morning, the girls coming straight from work to the coach. Initially as food was still rationed the girls were asked to take a small piece of cheese, butter and tea etc. with them. Many hosts refused these rations and one girl can remember a tin of sardines travelling all over Britain and remaining unopened.

The girls would leave Luton with their suitcases packed, not knowing where they would be sleeping that night. There were generally two coaches; the first one carried a board with "Luton Girls Choir on Tour" written on it, and there were two regular coach drivers, Wally Naish and Alf Aynscombe. A third driver joined them later on. While travelling the girls would talk, knit and sleep; Mr Davies did not like them to sing as he did not want their voices taxed before a concert. He also did not want noisy coaches travelling through the countryside; however on this point he was often overruled and especially on the second coach the girls would be led in their singing by Yvonne James. In the end Mr Davies bought her a harmonica. As well as the established songs the girls sang their own song to the tune of "She Wears Red Feathers". (See appendices)

On arrival at the venue there would be tea, followed by a rehearsal. In 1949 the firm of R Colin Large made a rostrum in five sections which could be transported fairly easily. This was conveyed by lorry to some of the venues and was assembled on flat stages so that the girls could be tiered. In churches they had to improvise and the girls would often be precariously standing on forms and chairs placed round the communion rail and pulpit. At halls where there were curtains the girls assembled quietly on the staging behind the scenes but if it was an open arrangement with the staging and piano on view, the girls would line up in the correct order out of sight and walk silently in two lines, one from each side, to their places, meeting in the middle. The girls normally stood on stage in approximately the same place, sopranos left of centre, mezzos upper right and contraltos lower right. Mr Davies always checked acoustically that the balance was correct and occasionally he shuffled them around.

After the concert the girls would wait in the hall, their names would be read out like war time refugees and they would be "claimed" and taken home by the hosts, to be given free bed and breakfast and often supper. Girls were normally billeted in pairs but if there was only room for one, then an older girl would go on her own. Today this arrangement probably would not be allowed and accommodation would increase the cost of touring beyond the reach of a similar choir.

The accommodation obviously varied; one week the girls could be in a well to do household with a maid waiting at table, the next in a small terraced house. They were also dependent on the host for food. When the girls finished the concert, they went home with their host and might or might not get supper. As they would only have had sandwiches since lunch time, they could be quite hungry. The majority of hosts were very welcoming and many girls made friends all over the country. They would stay with the same people each time.

There are many stories connected with "digs". Very occasionally, although vetted, the digs were not all that could be desired and the girls were moved. On the first tour, Connie Chandler and her friend actually had breakfast with a man and a boy wanted by the police and had to "help with enquiries".

Josie Driscoll and her friend Doreen were amazed when their hosts drove through enormous gates to a very large house, which was actually an Old Peoples Home converted from a workhouse. Their hosts had private rooms but in the morning Doreen went in her night-dress down the wrong corridor to the bathroom. The old people were quite surprised to see her.

Peggy Coggins recalls her stay with two elderly ladies in Eastbourne who before going to bed said "we must have our medicine". Visualising something like "Syrup of figs" Peggy was relieved when she was offered a Pontefract Cake. The next morning the two ladies came into her bedroom in procession, one carrying a tray of early morning tea with chocolate biscuits and the other a big shawl with which she enveloped Peggy. She also had a bottle of aspirins. Happily it was nothing sinister. They just thought she might have a headache after her late night.

Deborah Gibson and her friend stayed with a couple who worked in and lived over an underwear shop. The way to the bathroom was through the couple's bedroom so she spent most of the night wanting to "go" but not daring to. When they were ready to leave the man presented each of them with a pair of knickers. Deborah's had a kangaroo on the front, the other girl had a frilly pair.

Of course boys were always interested in the girls and Deborah can remember one of her host's two boys being very disappointed that their mum had got two of the young ones. The boys said "Goodbye" before the girls had even sat down.

Sandra Goodman remembers two episodes connected with food from the late '60s. In Sutton-in-Ashfield Sandra and her friend Janice were billeted with a lady who did not attend the concert. She had however prepared a large meal for them afterwards and when they arrived, she went to bed and left them to it. The custard had not set and there were no spoons, it took them a long time to eat it using the base of a fork. There was much giggling, although the girls did try to be quiet as the lady's bedroom was attached to the lounge. It was all rather a challenge.

In Ipswich she stayed with a family whose father was a bit of a joker. He said he had been told the girls would be hungry after the concert and would require a light snack. Leaving the room, he then came back with a tray of light bulbs!

The same weekend Alison Nicol and her friend were staying at digs in the country and when they were ready to go the host's car would not start. They all tried pushing it but eventually had to have a tow before the car would go. The next morning while out for a walk, although not in uniform they were recognised by a member of the audience from the concert the previous evening. He stopped his car to tell the girls how much he had enjoyed their singing.

In the early days the bedrooms would often be cold but there was nearly always a hot water bottle in the bed and coats served as an extra blanket. Occasionally the girls would stay in hotels or guests houses. At Bournemouth when it was a weekend tour the Choir were always in a hotel; this once caused problems as the local male population could be persistent followers.

On Sunday the girls would be taken back to the concert venue to board the coach. It was then on to the next town for lunch before they sang. Lunch might be in a hall or with a host family. One morning the girls asked Peggy what they were having for lunch and she replied "Dick Deadeye Pie". To her surprise when they arrived at the restaurant it looked as if her joke might have misfired, as they were to have lunch over an undertaker's premises. As the girls got off the coach many were saying "I don't think I want any lunch".

Anne Norcross can remember going with her friend to a home with a large family. They all sat down and were given an enormous Yorkshire pudding covered in gravy. This was followed by a Christmas lunch, turkey and trimmings and then the Christmas pudding. After this the girls had to sing! She does not know how she got through the concert feeling so ill and made a note not to eat so well again.

The Sunday concert would often be in a church and the programme would feature some semi sacred songs. Tea would be provided at the church and could vary from the elaborate to the rather meagre. By this time the girls were anxious to be on their way home rather than eating curled up sandwiches and the girl giving the "Thank you speech" would often feel her colleagues mentally hurrying her along.

The coaches would be back in Luton about 10pm. On the return journey some of the girls would be putting on make up for a quick meeting with their boy friends who would meet the coach and walk the girls home. Other members would be pinning up their hair ready for bed to save time when they got back. In the early years the coach would drop the girls on the main roads and they would make their own way home or be met by parents. Later parents met the coach in Alma Street. This caused some problems as at least one mother was questioned by police as to why she was waiting in her car at that time of night!

When going away for concerts Mr Davies parked his car in Barrett's Showroom at the bottom of Castle Street. On return, often in the middle of the night, he would unlock the garage, put on all the lights, drive out into the road and then re lock the garage. He would then give some of the girls a lift home.

The girls had to be back at work or school the next day, regardless of what time they arrived home the night before. They all had to write "Thank you" letters to their hosts as well.

When the Choir were singing in London they would sometimes have their meals in Lyons Corner House in an area specially put aside for them. Weekend and Bank Holiday tours could be fitted in around the working girl's normal time off, but the week long visits were taken from the girl's holiday entitlement. This was yet another sacrifice of spare time to the Choir.

During their time of touring the girls would collect a charm from each town they visited and these would be fixed onto a bracelet and worn at concerts. When the girls raised their hands to sing, there would be a chinking noise as the charms knocked together.

Over the years various parents were involved with the touring, some as transport managers, others as general helpers. Mrs Davies chaperoned the girls but Mr Davies invited individual sets of parents along to help with the luggage and any problems which might occur while the Choir was away. Edna Broughall can remember her father helping with transport and keeping an eye on the girls. She felt, as a father of four girls, he knew how to be kind but firm.

In 1951 the Choir's method of transport itself made the news when they started to use two new Leyland coaches. A feature in one of the papers described the coaches as having the last word in luxury fittings. There was a clear view scenic sunroof and the coaches were 6 inches wider than normal, with larger seats and more leg room.

The girls were only stranded once. On a trip to Worthing in 1968 the roads were flooded and the coaches were unable to leave. Mr Davies had to make an appeal for overnight accommodation and the girls returned to Luton on the Monday.

When travelling became easier parents would often follow the Choir, either in a special coach or individually by car. They would spend the weekend at the seaside, attending the concert in the evening. Parents and possibly any boy friends who also went along, would stay in hotels in the area.

As the road network improved over the years it became much easier to make longer journeys and the Choir could do more "one night" concerts. They did however continue to do the National Children's Home tours until the Choir finished.

A wider audience

On Sunday June 13th 1946, the Choir went to Clacton and gave two performances in the Concert hall of the Corporation Band Pavilion, one of the largest and most up to date in the country. The Band of the Beds and Herts Regiment were with them and when the hall was full for the afternoon concert the summer auditorium was opened and 300 - 400 people were able to listen in there. The evening performance was also oversubscribed, it started at 8pm but by 6pm people were already queuing. The cafe adjoining the hall was opened to accommodate a further 300 but many were turned away.

The Choir were invited to return for a week in September but Mr Davies said this would be impossible; he would however arrange a three day weekend. So it was Clacton again in September. They left Luton on the Friday and had a concert that evening as well as singing on Saturday and Sunday, the last programme being compered by Ronnie Waldman. The guest artiste that evening was R Colin Large, one of Luton's councillors who later became Mayor. He often travelled with the Choir on tour and sang in their concerts.

The Westminster Central Hall was the setting for a concert in October 1946 when the Choir were accompanied by the Band of the Coldstream Guards. The organ was played by Dr G. Thalben Ball and on the trumpet was Mr Davies' boyhood friend the local and renowned band conductor Harry Mortimer. In the audience with the Earl and Countess of Gowne and Air Marshall Sir Arthur Coningham was the Duchess of Kent, President of the Primrose League which was benefiting from the concert. After the show she asked the girls if they minded her having tea with them. As Grace Crew said, "Mind! we welcomed her." The Duchess was charming, putting the girls at their ease and chatting quite happily. She then thanked the girls for allowing her to join them and left them feeling thrilled to have met and talked with such a lovely lady.

In March 1947 Mr Davies and Harry Mortimer were together again, this time in a broadcast from Luton, when an audience of 1,000 people as well as the radio listeners heard the Choir singing with their local band in a new series called "Saturday Bandstand". It was recorded at the Central Mission Hall Midland Road.

The end of March saw the Choir in Coventry, their arrival being announced by loudspeakers in the streets. They received a Civic Reception from the Lord Mayor in the Council Chambers where he shook hands with each girl as she was introduced by Mr Davies; the Mayoress was amongst those who waited on the girls at tea.

Their evening concert was at the Central Hall to a very appreciative audience. The final number "Someday We Shall Meet Again" received four encores, the audience still applauding while the girls were singing.

The night was spent in Coventry and on the Sunday morning while out walking, the girls visited the ruined Cathedral. In the shadow of the charred wooden cross they spontaneously sang one of their songs. A sizeable crowd gathered and the girls felt very moved by a memorable happening recalled by one of the girls as something special, even so long afterwards. In the afternoon they moved on to Leamington Spa for a concert in the Pump Room.

April 1947 also saw the start of a tradition, Clacton for Easter. The girls arrived on Good Friday but only gave two concerts on the Sunday; the rest of the time they were on holiday. During the evening performance the audience were asked to vote on 11 items for inclusion in the second half. The guest artiste was again R Colin Large.

By April the Choir had made 14 broadcasts in the previous 15 months and perhaps as an omen for 1948, in May 1947 a Royal Command. Queen Mary asked for the Choir to sing in the BBC Broadcast for her 80th birthday. It was a Gala Variety Show, part of an evening of music. Introduced by Richard Murdoch and Kenneth Horne it also featured Elsie and Doris Waters, Tommy Handley and Anne Ziegler and Webster Booth.

The BBC's 25th Anniversary was in November 1947 with a week of celebrations from the 9th to the 16th culminating with a two hour show, live from His Majesty's Theatre. The show featured Charlie Chester and his Gang, The Radio Revellers, Vera Lynn, Eric Barker, Pearl Hackney, Vic Oliver, Tommy Handley and Co. and many other household names. Amongst this glittering array were the Luton Girls Choir. Each act introduced the one following and it fell to 13 year old Pamela Smith to announce Vic Oliver. She was one of the "babies" of the Choir and had first started as a speaker for the Choir 10 months ago at Watford. This was her first "speaking" broadcast and although "scared stiff" she did it very professionally.

At the end of 1947 the Choir's friend Richard Tauber was in hospital. While the girls were in London for a broadcast, Mr Davies asked two of them to visit St Thomas's and leave a card and some fruit for the star. The girls expected to leave the gifts at reception but they were asked to wait and within minutes, at Richard Tauber's invitation, they were taken to meet him in his private ward. He shook hands, asked them what the Choir was doing in London and talked of future plans, saying that he would be singing with them the following February.

Unfortunately on February 20th 1948 the Choir was singing at his Memorial Concert in the Royal Albert Hall. Ronnie Waldman had originally brought them together and he asked the girls to sing "You are my Heart's Delight" as he felt

Richard Tauber would have appreciated that. They sang it in the second half with Elizabeth Schwarzkopf and Herbert Dawson and were conducted by Walter Goehr. They opened the first half with Mozart's "Alleluia" and also sang "My Heart and I", conducted by George Melachrino. The BBC Theatre Orchestra played and Rawicz and Landauer and Sir Adrian Boult also took part in the concert.

On February 1st 1948 the British Film Festival took place at the Odeon Cinema Leicester Square, when the Daily Mail Film Awards were presented. The idea was to feature short scenes from the films shown the previous year and then ask people to send in votes for their favourite picture and stars, to the Daily Mail offices. The Choir was the first organisation outside the British Film Industry to take part in the Festival and they sang a selection of "music made by the movies" accompanied by the Orchestra directed by Sydney Torch. The show started with a scene from "It Always Rains on Sunday" starring Googie Withers and Jack MacCallam and ended with John Mills and Valerie Hobson in "Great Expectations". Also appearing on stage were Jean Kent, Valerie Hobson, Anna Neagle and Margaret Lockwood.

There was an audience of 2,000 people in the theatre and many more heard the show on the radio. The girls went to the theatre early for rehearsals and then sat and watched the stars perform; this was another chance to collect many autographs. One girl remembers two of the stars coming to blows, punching and pulling each other's hair. They had to be separated, a different view of the stars.

The Choir appeared twice more at the Festival, in 1949 and 1950. In 1949 when the girls sang "Dream of Olwen", the programme included scenes from "The Red Shoes" starring Moira Shearer, "Brighton Rock" with Richard Attenborough and William Hartnell, and "My Brother Jonathan" with Dulcie Gray and Michael Dennison. At rehearsal the Choir enjoyed meeting Anna Neagle and Michael Wilding who later featured in "Spring in Park Lane".

Members of the Choir at the 1949 Film Festival with Anna Neagle and Michael Wilding.
Photo from Library Collection.

The following year the Choir sang one of the songs from the film "The Glass Mountain". Michael Dennison and Dulcie Gray performed their scene and then Tito Gobbi sang "The Song of the Mountains". Meanwhile the Choir stood in the middle of the stage in front of a backcloth featuring the Alps. They were hidden by a gauze curtain which then dropped and the Choir sang "Take the Sun". Years later Anne Norcross was on holiday in Spain and met a lady who had been a cashier at the Odeon cinema. She remembered the night clearly, a lovely scene with the girls in their blue dresses and the white Alps in the background.

Easter 1948 was again at Clacton. R Colin Large sang "The Fisherman of England" at the Sunday afternoon concert which was a sell out. 400 people were in the summer auditorium and a cafe was especially closed to hold another audience. The concert was broadcast to them over a relay system.

The Choir nearly always sang during the service at the Trinity Methodist Church on the Easter Sunday morning, probably because of the National Children's Home and Methodist connection. Also many of their hosts were members of the congregation. Saturday evening concerts in the Town Hall were lighter programmes and although they still contained some more serious music, they were more relaxed and fun. The presentation however was still of a high quality.

The girls sometimes got a bit fed up with every Easter at Clacton although they enjoyed being by the sea. They often stayed with the same families and later some of the girls went back to spend holidays with people who ran a guest house just for folk they knew. Grace Crew met her future husband there; he was a guest at the same time as the Choir. When they later married there was a leading column and a photograph in the East Essex Gazette. The heading being "Hospital Security marries Luton Girls Choir Girl". Twenty of the girls would stay in a small hotel where the sons of the house would make up "apple pie" beds, putting hair brushes and such things for the girls to find.

The girls were not allowed to roam around the town; Mr Davies said they were ambassadors of Luton and should conduct themselves as such. They were not supposed to visit Butlin's Holiday Camp fairground but of course they did. Marie Robinson can remember the thrill of hearing the Choir's records being played on the fairground juke boxes and one year two of the girls went on the big wheel which broke down. It was pouring with rain and the girls arrived late for a concert. Mrs Davies was waiting in the wings with their dresses and they were in big trouble with Mr Davies after the show. Some girls spent their money at the ice skating rink so they all did manage to enjoy the "off duty" time.

Luton firms had played a big part in the war effort, one of the items produced by Vauxhall being the Churchill tank. In June 1948 Mr Churchill came to the town and on a beautifully sunny day in the morning, he walked along George Street to thank the people of Luton for their efforts. He then had lunch at the George Hotel before driving to a fete at Luton Hoo, organised by the Eastern Area Conservative and Unionist Associations. As he appeared the Choir sang "Land of Hope and Glory".

Special trains were run from London, East Anglia and the Midlands and 100,000 people listened to Mr Churchill's rousing speech and enjoyed various entertainers including Richard Murdoch and Kenneth Home.

Trustees

In 1947 as the Choir were becoming more popular and more money was involved, Mr Davies felt that people would think he was doing quite well out of running the Choir. To safe-guard his name it was decided to form a Board of Trustees to deal with the financial side and on Saturday July 5th the first meeting was held in the Mayor's parlour in the Town Hall. The original Trustees were Councillor R Colin Large, Alderman George Seaward, Mr Rex Parrott and Mr Stuart Broughall. The Honorary Treasurer was Mr A.R. Hills and the Legal Advisor was Mr P.R.Barnard.

The idea was to have a Trustee to represent the Town Council, one to represent the people of Luton and two to represent the girls. Honorary publicity officer was John Gibbs, Chairman of the Home Counties Newspaper group.

The officers changed over the years and people who later served included Mr R. R. Hopkins, Mr Douglas Biart, Mr H.G.Chichester Miles, Mr Robert Janes, Mr Hedley Gore, Mr R.T.A Singer and Mr A.J.D.Langford.

The Trustees acted as a buffer between the public and Mr Davies, keeping his profile as the genial man that appeared before the audience. Behind the scenes he could be difficult as he was very single minded as far as furtherance of the Choir and music was concerned. After the success of the Australasian Tour, for example, the Choir were asked to go to South Africa and Mr Davies was keen to go. However there was a national feeling against apartheid especially amongst show and sports people and the Trustees felt it would be difficult to obtain leave of absence for the girls if their employers were of a similar mind. They advised against the Choir going although a promotional tape had been made and two offers for a tour were received in 1961. An offer was again made in 1969 but the Luton Council of Churches and the Fabian Society were still opposed.

Later, because the Trustees technically held the legal right to appoint the Musical Director, they were able to hold the Choir in suspension and so prevent its take over by any another person when Mr Davies was taken ill.

Chapter Four

The Command Performance

Monday 1st of November 1948 was a real "red letter" day for members of the Choir. This was when they appeared in the Royal Command Performance at the London Palladium, in aid of the Variety Artistes Benevolent Fund, the only time that an amateur organisation had appeared in the programme.

Each of the established members had their own personal invitation; it was not just a block booking for the Luton Girls Choir. As there were a few extra places available, the names of the new girls were put into a hat at rehearsal and the lucky ones were chosen by Mr Alec Webb, one of the parents. Two of these were Josie Fisher and Doreen Rawlings.

On the Saturday evening 60 girls went to London with Mr Davies to appear in the radio programme "In Town Tonight". Pamela Smith, the 14 year old commere was interviewed and the Choir sang "O Lovely Night". They all returned to Luton that night ready for a Civic send off the following morning.

The Mayor and Members of the Council were in the chamber at 9.30 am. on the Sunday morning to wish the girls "Good Luck", the Mayor shaking the hand of each girl as they boarded the coach for London. There was one girl, Stella Parrott, bitterly disappointed to be left at home, unable to go because she was unwell. The Choir stayed in London on the Sunday and Monday nights at the National Hotel, Bedford Way, Russell Square and parents were given a card with the hotel details on, in case they needed to contact their daughter. The girls all had single rooms with their own keys. One of them remembers it as a completely new experience - a glimpse of a different way of life with the elegant place settings for meals, all those knives and forks. For this special occasion the Choir had new blue dresses with white lace collars and white buckskin shoes; the latter were stiff and hurt according to one member but that was a small price to pay.

There were five hours of rehearsals on the Sunday and Monday. Girls were told that anybody late for rehearsals would not be able to take part in the show, a dire warning guaranteed to ensure punctuality. No talking was allowed during the rehearsals but the Choir were able to sit in the stalls watching the other performers rehearsing and chatting to the great names also appearing, people like Danny Kaye, Julie Andrews, Ted Ray and Arthur Askey.

On the Monday night, mounted police escorted the coach along Great Marlborough Street through cheering crowds. In the dressing room Mr Davies read out "Good Luck" telegrams from many well wishers including the Crazy Gang, Doris Arnold, Harry Pepper and the Band of the Irish Guards. As the Choir waited on stage for the curtain to rise other stars mingled amongst them, offering congratulations and encouragement.

On the steps of Luton Town Hall before leaving for the Command Performance. Photo Luton News.

Borough of Luton

Scientiæ et Labori Detur

At the Meeting of the Council held on Tuesday, 28th December, 1948, it was Resolved Unanimously:–

That this Council place on record their appreciation of the very high standard of the performances given by the members of the

Luton Girls' Choir,

under the able and inspiring leadership of their Conductor, Mr. Arthur E. Davies, at the numerous public appearances in Luton and other towns and through the medium of broadcasting; that the Council offer warm congratulations to the Choir on being selected to appear at the Royal Command Performance on the 1st November, 1948, which they consider was a well-deserved honour conferred in recognition of the outstanding merit and popular appeal of the Choir's renderings of choral music and brought credit not only to themselves but to Luton itself; and that the Council tender to the Choir their sincere good wishes for their success in the future and the hope that for many years they will continue to receive the support of lovers of good music.

W. J. Edwards. Mayor

W. H. Robinson Town Clerk

The Illuminated Address presented to the Choir after their appearance in the Royal Command Performance. Photo Bob Norman.

They were on stage for about 5 minutes. Stewart McPherson introduced them and a net curtain, which was draped across the stage, parted to reveal the Choir. They sang "Break of Day" accompanied by the Melachrino Strings and then "Freedom" by Roger Quilter. Joan Folks remembers a special feeling at the end when all the performers stood on stage, the lights went up and they all turned to face the Royal Box. The producer of the show, Mr Charles Henry, said of the Choir "They took their places worthily among all the other stars and did all that was expected of them. They fell into the production scene just like old performers".

Afterwards there was a reception at the Palm Court where the girls were allowed to mingle with the stars and collect autographs. They also waxed lyrical over the food.

These "stars" were back as ordinary girls the next day, either at school or work. They were exhausted but "on a high" for days. Everyone they met wanted to hear about their experiences. It cost the Choir about £600 to attend but was considered to be well worth it and the expense was recouped through a series of concerts.

1948 was an extremely busy and successful year for the Choir. They had made their first record for Parlophone and by November there were three. They were heard regularly on the radio, being paid 15 guineas for a thirty minute slot and at one time the Choir were singing every week on "Monday Night at Eight". They would receive the music on Friday to rehearse and be ready to sing it on the programme on Monday. The Choir would meet in Bridge Street after work or school and set off for London by coach, not the deluxe model of today; as the coach was not heated, each girl had a grey army blanket to wrap herself in when it got cold. There were no motorways and the journey took much longer than it would today.

Tea was a box containing two sandwiches, probably made a lot earlier in the day, and a cake. It was off to London for the recording and afterwards down to the basement for a cup of pea soup in the BBC canteen. According to some of the girls the food was bad even in those days.

A report in the Luton News described the second recording session for the Scarlet and Blue first series of radio broadcasts. - Two cream coloured coaches leave Bridge Street Luton on a Wednesday evening filled with the Luton Girls Choir for the BBC recording studios at Maida Vale.

No time for a cup of tea when they arrive and 10 minutes later they are in studio 1, the Choir on one side, the band on the other and rehearsals had begun. Stops and starts, frequent at first as the two conductors, with another Luton man Harry Mortimer, discuss technical angles.

After 90 minutes the three men are satisfied. The producer's voice says "Studio ready please, we start recording 10 seconds from now". Then the signature tune "Music in My Heart" played by the band and sung by the Choir blend and rise. "This is the BBC Light Programme" comes from the announcer. A false start and they start again. Half an hour later and the programme is finished. The programme had overrun by a minute and a half and alterations have to be made. Another run through of the last part of the programme, producer Harry Mortimer is satisfied".

During those early years the Choir appeared in Alhambra of the Air, Children's Hour, Christmas Cracker, Jubilee Variety, Monday Night at Eight, Saturday Bandstand and Variety Bandbox. They had been interviewed on In Town Tonight and also heard on the General Overseas Network.

They had sung in nine big concerts in London and appeared at five of London's largest theatres, the Coliseum, His Majesty's, Golders Green Hippodrome, The Scala and Winchmore Hill Capitol.

It was also in 1948 that Marion Jones began her 9 year run in the radio programme "Chapel in the Valley". She had been "discovered" by Sandy Macpherson when he was hosting a concert at which Marion had sung a solo. Chapel in the Valley was a "land of let's pretend", a little visit to a chapel in the heart of the country where the village postmaster was the organist and the choir leader was Mr Edwards, a farmer. Marion was chosen to play his daughter but the cast were anonymous, the nearest to identification being the information that his daughter was played by a member of the Luton Girls Choir.

Chapter Five

Recording

When the Choir started to make records it was a new venture for them all. As they were amateurs it was difficult to get them all together in the day time, so recording had to be done in the evening during the week. This meant the girls had to go to London straight from school or work and did not get home until late. It also meant the recording had to be done in one session so the singing had to be right; the songs were always well rehearsed beforehand.

When the Choir made a recording it was not quite the same sound as at their concerts, and in recordings the Choir were accompanied by an orchestra, often that of George Melachrino. Mr Davies was behind the screens looking at recording machines, not in front of the Choir as he would be at a concert.

The Choir's first records were for the Parlophone Company and were made at studios in St. John's Wood. Prior to the girls' first recording trip, Mr Davies, ever the perfectionist, wrote them all one of his letters.

Very important points connected with gramophone recording.

1) Accept every required detail and finesse, without becoming frustrated.

2) Be absolutely quiet throughout the whole session, with no hilarity whatsoever.

3) Do not distract the attention of the girl either side of you.

4) Suppress all coughs. (very valuable material is wasted if coughing is prevalent while reproduction is in progress).

5) On arrival be very attentive to all instructions, and get to your places quickly in the order in which I shall place you, which may be different from which we are accustomed.

6) Do not scrape your feet on the floor. Do not even admire your new shoes at the wrong time.

7) If you have a "break" during the session, walk quietly away from the stage.

8) If you get "browned off", do not show or remark on it.

9) Aim at being the most efficient and business like amateur organisation in the country.

So much for the generalities. I want now to refresh your memory on important matters of technique.

Tone.

Refine every note please. Nothing harsh, severe or square.

Colour. Variation is vital. Endeavour to give all light and shade possible. Will appreciate grand pianissimo singing, with perfect diction and articulation.

Pitch.

This heading should perhaps have come first on the list, for I can not sufficiently

In a recording studio. Photo from Library Collection.

stress the importance of singing "dead in tune". Allow your ear to be sensitive to exact chording. Listen while you sing. Your tendency is sharpness, so unlike advice to middle aged folk, will you on ascending passages not overstep the intervals, but on descending, do the opposite; in fact rather exaggerate them. To sum up this point contraltos and mezzos should make sure that they are under the note, while sopranos should not be above the note.

Diction and Pronunciation

The only thing about Luton of which I can not be proud is its "brogue". No broad vowels please, and make perfectly certain that second syllables of words containing open vowels are less prominent.

Articulation.

Let the experts hear all your Ds and Ts at the end of the words, and artistically roll your Rs.

Breathing.

This must be truly diaphragmatical. Do not use undue pressure of breath when singing fortissimo. Naturally and silently fill the diaphragm, and open and shape the mouth as you have been taught.

The possibilities of future commercial recording relies upon tonight's efforts, but above all be confident, artistic and painstaking. **You can do it.**

P S. From the contraltos I want a very deep warm tone **please**. Nothing "white". We must hear you, especially in records, as I still have a feeling that in reproduction of broadcasts there is still too much "top".

The girls obviously got it right. By November 1948 there were 3 Choir records listed in the Parlophone Record Bulletin and a picture of the Choir featured on the front cover. Their records were:- 1) My Heart and I and You are my Heart's Delight. 2) Count Your Blessings and Break of Day 3) Silent Night and The Holy Child, this being their latest release.

Count Your Blessings was constantly being played on the radio, especially on "Housewife's Choice" and together with Break of Day sold 63,000 copies in its first year. By 1949 one of the "Bulletins" carried a whole page advert for the Choir's new record, together with three photographs of the Choir in action. Their latest release was Trees by Kilner-Rasbach arr by Harris, and Serenata arr by A.E Davies. Apart from the new one and the three from 1948 the Choir had made four other records, Easter Hymn and The Blue Danube Waltz, The Dream of Olwen and Barcarolle from the Tales of Hoffmann, Your Prayers are Asked and I Heard a Robin Singing and Till all our Dreams come True and While the Angelus was Ringing. Royalties from all the record sales greatly enhanced the Choir's funds.

In 1950 Mr Davies thought it would be a nice idea for each of the soloists who had given more than 5 years loyal service, to make a record on their own as a souvenir of their time with the Choir. The Trustees agreed to fund this and a collection towards the cost was also made at one of the concerts. Six lucky singers and pianists Eileen Gaskin and Mollie Litchfield cut their own discs, courtesy of Parlophone records. Three copies of each were made, Mr Davies had one and the girls had the other two. Betty Bird had one of hers framed like future "pop stars" did with their gold discs.

By 1951 there were 16 Choir records available. Not all of these had been made in the studio, as the Choir also recorded elsewhere. Sometimes this was successful as when the Choir sang at St. Paul's Cathedral in May 1950. They had recorded the "Shepherd's Cradle Song", accidentally picking up the sound of a baby crying. As this had actually enhanced the song it was left in the recording. In July 1951 they were not quite so lucky. 85 girls together with part of Phil Green's Concert Orchestra, visited Black Park Wood in Iver Buckinghamshire to record "Down in the Forest" by Landon Ronald. This was so that real bird song could be included. A motor trial was being held on the road near to where the recording was to be done but after some negotiations the organisers diverted the route. Nobody however could divert the cuckoo which kept joining in, in the wrong places, necessitating several retakes.

Betty Bird's Solo Record, framed in a similar fashion to the Pop Stars. Photo Bob Norman.

THE
LUTON GIRLS CHOIR
conducted by Arthur E. Davies
These are their Records

Records	
My heart is singing Such lovely things are these	R3356
Shepherd's Cradle Song Panis Angelicus (Recorded in St. Paul's Cathedral, London)	E11476
The clock is playing Charlie is my darling ; Skye Boat Song	R3339
My Lady Greensleeves (The beautiful month of May) I hear your voice	R3321
Take the sun (film : "The Glass Mountain") King's Rhapsody—Some day my heart will awake	R3293
Down in the glen Lift up your heart	R3276
Old Chelsea—Music in my heart Lisbon Story—Someday we shall meet again	R3253
Tales from the Vienna Woods O Lovely Night	R3223
Serenata (Toselli) Trees	R3212
Casanova—Nuns' Chorus The Holy City	E11470
Your prayers are asked I heard a robin singing	R3169
Dream of Olwen Tales of Hoffmann—Barcarolle	R3156
The Holy Child Silent Night, Holy Night	R3146
Count your blessings Break of day	R3118
Blue Danube Cavalleria Rusticana—Easter Hymn	E11464
Old Chelsea—My Heart and I Land of Smiles—You are my heart's delight	E11461

Complete list up to and including March 1951

NOTICE—Copyright subsists in PARLOPHONE records. Any unauthorised broadcasting, public performance, copying or re-recording of such records in any manner whatsoever will constitute an infringement of copyright and is forbidden. Applications for licences should be addressed to THE PARLOPHONE COMPANY, LTD., Hayes, Middlesex, England. PARLOPHONE records are also protected by patents in Great Britain, Eire and other countries ; any sale of such records at other than the authorised prices constitutes an infringement and renders the infringer liable to an action at law.

Printed in Great Britain B. & S., Ltd. PS585/251 Prices not valid in Eire

A publicity leaflet from "Parlophone" listing the Choir's recordings available in 1951. Photo Bob Norman.

The threat of "Rock and Roll" was looming in 1957 when Mr Davies announced at a Blue Rhapsody concert that there would be six records made under the Blue Rhapsody label. These would be for people who were lovers of well written light music and well loved classics. The records featured the Choir with the organist Felton Rapley FRCO ARCM, the songs included:- "Kindness" and "Song of a Thankful Heart", "The Lord's Prayer" and "There but for the Grace of God go I", "Christopher Robin is Saying his Prayers" and "The Shepherd's Cradle Song", "Praise my Soul the King of Heaven" and "Dear Lord and Father of Mankind", "Sun of my Soul" and "The Day Thou Gavest Lord is Ended", and "Panis Angelicus" and "He shall Feed His Flock". The records were 10ins in size, cost 6s.3½d and half the proceeds from the sales would go to the National Children's Home. They played at 78rpm. and were available from Blue Rhapsody Recordings 1-5 Portpool Lane, Holborn, London.

In 1959 a 12in LP record called "Devotion" including some of the above titles together with "Abide with Me", "The Lord is my Shepherd" and Schubert's "Omnipotence", was made especially for the Australasian Tour and only distributed in Australia by Columbia. Parlophone produced a 7in EP called "Maidens in Melody" with "Count Your Blessings" and "Break of Day" on one side and on the other was "Dream of Olwen" and "Barcarolle".

By 1961 the Choir had made 50 recordings; in its heyday it reflected the music of the era and Mr Davies's picture appeared on the sheet music of songs made famous by the Choir. That year the Royalties from "You are my Heart's Delight" totalled £1,375 and this all went to the Richard Tauber Memorial Scholarship fund, which had originally been started from money raised at Tauber's memorial concert. The Scholarship was awarded by the Anglo Austrian Music Society, formed in 1942, to promote and encourage appreciation, understanding and performance of British and Austrian Music. Also in 1961, their Jubilee Year, the Luton girls produced a record called "Souvenir - 25 Years of Music".

Things did not stay so rosy as other types of music strove for prominence. In March 1964 15,000 record sleeves on the Luton Girls Choir LP "Best Loved Songs" had to be withdrawn because the sleeve notes by Derek Johnson of Musical Express said "The Luton Girls Choir will evoke countless memories in the minds of every adult listener ... to the younger generation this Choir may have little or no signification since it no longer functions under this name". EMI said Mr Johnson was only given 24 hours to write the notes, because they were behind schedule.

This incorrect information was also picked up by the magazine "Education Extracts" which reviewed the record saying "Although this famous Choir is no longer with us and therefore is unknown to most children of school age, it is worth remembering that the Luton Girls Choir was unique - the leading choir of its type in Britain. Many other choirs tried to copy its example; yet none of them achieved half the fame and national admiration earned by the original. Fifteen years after reaching the apex of their popularity, these fresh, youthful voices are still requested by listeners to several radio record programmes. And the Choir's high standard of performance can still serve as an illustration wherever light choral singing is practised."

The record was actually a dubbing of 14 titles released originally on "78" between 1948 and 1951 and the company obviously thought the Choir was still a viable product.

It may have been because of this slip up that the sleeve notes for the compilation were rather "purple". "This is an album which positively oozes from every track. The Luton Girls Choir will evoke countless memories, for the songs in which they are featured are amongst the most outstanding in the treasure trove of all time favourites. Their 1948/9 recordings are now collectors' items, greatly sought after even by the younger generation, for this Choir, which has received world wide prestige since those early days, has a universal appeal to all age groups. Now, thanks to the miracle of modern recording techniques, it is possible to present on a modern disc 14 original tracks in all their unsurpassed freshness and clarity. All of these items are established favourites and are featured in current "live" concerts of the Choir whose present popularity can be measured by its 15 months ahead bookings.

During the dark days towards the end of the war, and the equally austere period which followed, the Luton Girls Choir helped to lighten our darkness with their captivating harmony. It was, indeed, the pioneer of many similar female choirs which sprang up in subsequent years.

Passing as we were through a particularly emotional phase, during which we grasped gladly and willingly at any shred of sentimentality or romanticism that presented itself, the Choir soared to a fantastic peak of popularity and its records sold in vast quantities, and although this was before the days of hit parades and best sellers, I am sure the girls would have made frequent appearances in the Top Twenty had it been in existence. If Top Twenty were given for frequency of demand in such programmes as Housewives' Choice or Family Favourites, the Luton Girls Choir would permanently top the Popular Request Chart."

Records were still produced in the later days, with a long playing record under the Music for Pleasure Label being made with the Rhapsody Chorus and the bands from the W.D. and H.O. Wills Brass Band Championship Concert in 1972. The Choir sang "The Gypsy Chorus", "The Hallelujah Chorus" and "Onward Christian Soldiers". In September 1974 the last record to be made by the Choir was recorded in the Priory Church Dunstable. Twelve titles of religious and classical music were issued by Chandos Promotions Ltd, recorded on the Contour/Polydor label. The "Rhapsody Chorus", present and former members, had one rehearsal on the 24th and then two recording sessions on the 25th and 26th.

The record was released in November and was first on sale when the Choir were singing at Pirton, Mr Davies happily autographing the copies sold. Girls could buy one copy at the performer's cost of 12/- (60p), an unlimited amount at the concessional rate of 15/- (75p) while the retail price was actually 17/6 (87p).

In 1975 Hedley Gore, one of the trustees, took a copy to New Zealand when he was on a trade mission. This was heard by Sir Robert Kerridge who had organised and backed the New Zealand part of the Choir's tour. He was still impressed with the Choir's singing and sent a cable to Mr Davies saying how much he had enjoyed the record.

Chapter Six

Dresses

When the girls were singing as the Ceylon Baptist Choir they had to provide their own white dresses and this meant they were all different lengths ranging from six to sixteen inches from the ground. Some girls wore white ankle socks, some black stockings. Mr Davies thought women standing in straight lines wearing long white "nightdresses" and holding their music in front of them, as was the custom with many choirs at that time, was very uninspiring, The first step to some uniformity was to standardise the length and provide dark blue sashes to wear over the dresses. One long suffering mother would take these sashes home to iron after each concert.

On becoming the Luton Girls Choir they continued to provide their own white dresses until December 1939, when at a concert in Chapel Street Methodist Church a uniform dress of white taffeta with a blue collar, cuffs and belt was first worn to celebrate the raising of £1000 for charity. These dresses were made by Alexander's of Wellington Street, Luton and Betty Bird can remember going there to be measured when she joined the Choir.

When a replacement was needed it was wartime and material was in short supply. It was decided to use white lace as this could be bought without using precious clothing coupons. The dress had pale blue piping on the collar, with buttoning to the waist and Patricia Corley can well remember her first concert at Park Town Methodist Church Luton, when as a little girl she was given her concert dress to wear. Pat's mother had not seen the Choir, so dressed her with the buttons down the back. Imagine Pat's embarrassment when she was told by one of the senior girls "you've got your dress on back to front".

Next came pale blue taffeta with a wide self colour belt and navy buttons and the legend "Girls in Blue" was born. The colour blue suited all girls - blond, brunette or redhead - and later was to prove a perfect foil for the uniforms of the military bands in their joint performances. For this dress the girls had reluctantly to surrender their clothing coupons.

Members were responsible for washing their own dresses and keeping them in good order. On leaving the Choir the dress was handed in and stored by the Wardrobe Mistress until issued to a new member. Younger girls could also exchange their dress for a larger size. Over the years the Wardrobe Mistresses were - Kathleen Morton, Joan Folks and Mary Davie. On her wedding day, Joan's guard of honour was formed by Choir girls making an archway of coat hangers. Eventually the wardrobe was transferred to the Choir office and the dresses and later the walking out uniforms were issued from there. When married, Joan again took on the job of alterations.

Mr Davies would tell the Wardrobe Mistress what was needed for the performance and she would pass the information on to the Choir.

After the war when material became more freely available, the next dress was of a thicker blue cotton in a different style. It had a sweetheart neckline with ruching at the bust and hips.

The replacement introduced in 1948 was again of blue cotton with a white lace collar and this was the dress worn for the Royal Command Performance. White shoes were provided and it was these which the girls thought were uncomfortable when they sang on that momentous occasion. The dress appeared in many of the photographs taken at that time, including the notable photo taken on the stage of the Alma Theatre, as well as the one featuring the Choir on the front cover of the Souvenir Brochure.

Until then all dresses had been made with short sleeves but one of the stage dresses made by Charles Butler in 1950 for the ill-fated American Tour was in pale blue Robia voile and had three quarter length sleeves; it fastened at the neck with a cherry red velvet bow. At the same time the Bata Shoe Company provided red shoes for the girls to wear. This particular dress was so suitable for packing that it maintained its popularity longer than any other and was taken on the Australasian Tour to be worn at the matinee performances. When the colour faded slightly due to constant washing it would be revived with a "blue bag" rinse. In the mid to late fifties when the "bouffant" look was so fashionable, paper nylon and frilly net waist slips were worn under these dresses.

To celebrate the great honour of being chosen to sing at the opening of the Festival Hall in 1951 there was a change of style. The dresses were still pale blue but in a type of linen material with a fitted bodice and a square neckline; soft draping was caught on the left shoulder with a dark red buckle. Soft unpressed pleats gave the necessary fullness to the skirt and the dresses were designed for ease of laundering and speed of change. In fact they proved rather disappointing as they creased badly and were worn only occasionally.

The same year, when television appearances were becoming more frequent, it was decided to introduce a Television Section comprising 36 of the more senior girls wearing full length gowns. Blue was not a good colour for television so they sang in evening dresses of old rose pink taffeta, quilted at the hem and with a diamante trim at the shoulder. Under these, the girls wore long pale pink waist slips frilled at the bottom; wine coloured lace mittens completed the outfit. The dresses were made locally by Mrs Napthine of Dunstable Road.

The dresses were not kept exclusively for television but were worn at concerts when this section would present "a spot" immediately after the interval, being placed in groups to form a picture, some sitting, some standing. The rest of the girls in blue then joined them for the remainder of the programme.

The girls did have trouble packing the dresses, especially when they had to pack their blue outfits as well.

The Choir at the Alma Theatre in Luton in the 1940's. Photo Luton News.

The Television Section at the New Opera House, Blackpool 1952. Photo from Library Collection.

The Highland Dancers. Photo David Sims of London (in the 1950's, now no record.)

Another feature introduced about this time was Scottish Dancing, by four members of the Choir in full Highland Dress. This was purchased from the Scotch House in London and the four girls were specially trained to dance the "Keel Row" to the Choir's vocal accompaniment.

The dress chosen for the full Choir in the late 1950's was ballerina length with a flattering cowl neckline and two panels at the back of the bodice. Made in soft nylon material it was also ideal as the main stage dress of the Australasian Tour. Being crease resistant for packing and drip dry for hasty laundering it stood the test for almost daily wear during the three months tour. Blue shoes specially dyed to match the dress were supplied by Norvic.

In 1963 when the weather was so cold, the girls were provided with white woollen stoles to wear over their dresses. These were very welcome when they were singing in some of the draughty buildings and churches with only moderate heating.

The final stage dress appeared in 1969 and was made by the California Dress Company of London. Full length, with sleeves to the wrist, it was in a nylon crepe material coloured "humming bird blue". Gold braid trimming matched the gold sandals.

Walking out uniform.

In 1951 each member was provided with a new showerproof coat of steel grey covet cloth, designed by Stone's Fashions. Gauging gave fullness at the back waistline and the skirt was gored, with roomy side pockets. There was a full lining of tartan wool plaid.

The following year the members asked if they could have a Luton Girls Choir blazer which they would pay for individually and also be at liberty to wear when not on official Choir duties. It was French navy with a pale blue badge on the pocket. This was specially designed to incorporate the Luton Corporation Coat of Arms as well as the Choir's title. The blazers were worn during the tour of Denmark.

The uniform of the 47 girls on the Australasian tour was decided by a girls' committee. To wear with the Choir blazer they had pale blue terylene skirts with accordion pleats. The skirts were made locally by Mangolds and even with the constant laundering, remained permanently pleated. White blouses, court shoes, gloves and berets completed the ensemble. The Luton Hat Manufacturers Association provided the beret as well as a soft brimmed hat for more formal occasions (not very popular with the girls and seldom worn). On arrival "down under" each girl was given another blouse of blue and white candy stripe material by an Australian manufacturer. As the tour was scheduled for early spring in that area and with the weather, particularly in New Zealand, being quite chilly, it was considered advisable to take a full length coat in a neutral beige or cream colour.

The Choir in their first long dresses, St Albans 1970. Photo from Library Collection.

Some of the girls in their "Walking Out Uniform" in Regents Park in 1964. Photo Luton News.

The Choir on the steps of Luton Town Hall in their "Walking Out Uniforms" 1964. Photo Luton News.

The official walking out uniform for the full Choir came into being in 1964 and when the Choir sang at the opening of the Queensway Hall in Dunstable the girls were upset because this was not ready. The supplier said the members had not gone to be measured in time. However when it did arrive they felt very smart in the light blue terylene skirts to wear with their French navy blue blazers. The skirts were again permanently pleated with a silver thread running down alternate pleats. The blouses, also of terylene, were pale blue gingham check and there were plain navy blue shoes to complete the outfit. The Parents Association helped with the cost of the skirts which later suffered during the "miniskirt" period when they were shortened by the girls and when the " long look" came in they were discarded.

Mr Davies was very strict about the girls having the correct items at concerts and many of them can remember their nightmares, when in their dreams they arrived at a concert without their dress or shoes. One girl dreamt that she sang in her underslip. The members of the Choir contributed to the cost of their dresses by paying a deposit which was refundable when the girl left. Contributions were also made during the years by the Parents and Supporters Association.

Chapter Seven

The Late Forties and America

A radio "picture" had been made of Luton and was broadcast in both Sweden and Denmark. Called "A Musical Industrial Town" it focused on the youth angle. A van toured the town recording interviews and activities, accompanied by Mr Totsten Jungstedt from Sweden and Mr Hesson Schmidt from Denmark. Two members of the Choir were interviewed. Mary Fordham who worked at Skefko had just left the Choir as she was about to get married, while at Vauxhall a current member, Joanne West, spoke to the reporters. The Mayor Councillor W.J. Edwards gave a short talk on Luton mentioning the Choir and the final destination was the Youth Head quarters in Waller Street to speak to Mr Davies and other youth leaders.

Easter 1949, as well as being Clacton, took in several other places; it was a very busy weekend for the girls. The Choir left Luton on Good Friday, appearing in Colchester's Moot Hall in the evening and singing to a large and appreciative audience, tickets for the concert having sold out within 36 hours. On Saturday the girls managed a boat trip before singing in the packed Town Hall that night. Sunday morning found them at Clacton Trinity Methodist Church where the Choir sang "Land of our Birth". They had earned their free afternoon which was followed by an evening performance at the Princes Theatre.

After lunch on Monday they left Clacton for London with a lot of singing still to do. First to the BBC studios for a rehearsal of "Hello Paris" which was being broadcast later that night. It was then on to the Harringay Arena where they appeared in the same concert as Paul Robeson, ending the first half of the programme with a twenty minute performance, singing four items. This was billed as "twenty minutes with England's ambassadors of song". To one of the girls, Harringay seemed a huge venue somewhat bigger than the Albert Hall, possibly because of its shape. She thought the presentation was more artistic than the shows there today.

The Choir then made a hasty retreat to the coach for the journey back to Broadcasting House while Mr Davies returned to the stage to accept the applause on their behalf. A note on the programme explained that the Choir was going to sing in the Paris - London link called "Hello Paris".

While on the coach the girls listened to the Light programme concert in which they were to take part and on their arrival at the studio they sang "The Dream of Olwen". Back into the coach and they arrived in Luton at 11pm on Easter Monday night; some were then at work on the Tuesday. All this on a holiday! The same girl's comment on her Easter break: "It must have been a very hectic weekend but that was usual in those days. Hectic but enjoyable sums it up I think".

Friday May 20th was the Choir's first appearance on TV when they featured in "Music Hall". They had not appeared before due to lack of space in the studios. The girls were at Alexandra Palace by 7pm for rehearsals before the show at 9.30 pm and the BBC estimated that the audience was over one million viewers.

Maybe it was their TV appearance which made the concert in Tunbridge Wells so popular. Tradition had it that the Assembly rooms were only half full for a Sunday concert but when the Choir sang, people were standing at the back of the hall and many had been unable to get tickets.

It was in 1949 that the girls of the Choir became film stars for a while, as the Choir of St. Mildred's School, starring in the film "Old Mother Riley, Headmistress". They were taken to the studios at Walton-on-Thames on 2 or 3 weekends and on one journey, when running late, had to change into their dresses on the coach. The studio was a cold great barn of a place and the girls had to rehearse many times before they pleased Arthur Lucan. Their first scene was in the schoolroom, where they wore their own dresses and sang "I Heard a Robin Singing". In the school sports day scene they were given sashes saying "St Mildred's School" which were worn over their concert dresses and they sang "Till all our Dreams Come True". The teacher was Kitty MacShane who was Old Mother Riley's daughter in the film; Mr Davies did not appear. After singing at the sports day the girls had to go out into the grounds to meet their film parents, played by "extras". One girl, Pat Griffin, was also lucky enough to play a small role in the film.

The film had its premiere in July 1950 at the Luton Gaumont Theatre. The Mayor, R Colin Large, introduced the Choir saying it had taken 23 hours for them to do their small bit in the film. The tune "Break of Day" started to play and the curtain drew back to reveal rows of the Choir. They sang a selection of songs including the two from the film and a new song by Mantovani called "Such Lovely Things are These". Finishing with "Someday we Shall Meet Again" everybody then settled down to enjoy the film.

Whitsun 1949, June 4th and 5th found the Choir in the "Land of Song". On the Saturday they were in Cardiff where they received a Civic welcome from the Lord Mayor Alderman T.S. Kenigan. He said he followed them on the radio and enjoyed listening to them but they would need to be on their mettle as it was their first time in Wales. The concert was in Cardiff City Hall and the first half ended with "The Easter Hymn". The singing was obviously of the best because the Lord Mayor stood up in appreciation. He was followed by the rest of the audience and later said he had been so moved by the Choir's rendering of the song.

At the end of the performance the Mayoress presented Edna Broughall with her retirement clock; she had been Music Librarian for 7 years and was singing in her last concert. Her fiance was in the audience and told her later that he had never heard the Choir sing so brilliantly. They obviously wanted to prove to the Welsh people that Luton girls could sing well too.

That evening the Choir travelled to Penarth where they spent the night, before

On the film set for the film "Old Mother Riley, Headmistress" 1949. Photo from Library Collection.

going on to Aberdare for the Sunday concert. The Choir were guests of the Trecyon Ladies Choir who joined them in singing three numbers during the concert and also entertained the guests with their singing during tea. The Welsh ladies had sold all the concert tickets very quickly and could have filled the hall three times over. They tried to arrange an extra performance but were unable to do so and about 600 people were disappointed.

During the tea afterwards the Choir had to sit through 11 speeches listening to various Welsh people boasting about Welsh singing, but the welcome was genuine. The Welsh ladies and their friends supplied all the food from their own stores, giving up their valuable food ration points. They also did all the preparation and waited on the tables, which was appreciated by all.

The Choir continued to tour during the summer of 1949, singing at Bexhill in June and appearing with the Western brothers and Kay Cavendish at Eastbourne in July. They proved to be the biggest box office draw at Folkestone's Leas Cliff Hall when 1,200 people packed the venue and 300 were turned away.

At this time the Choir were appearing on Radio Luxembourg, recording programmes at Elstree studios as well as recording locally for the BBC. The latter was not without problems. On July 4th during a programme from the Central Mission in Luton the landline broke three times, and the Choir were then asked to record a further 25 minutes to be broadcast the following Tuesday. One of the soloists was suffering from the heat and was sick 10 minutes before the show, but she insisted on singing before going home. Both the shows were also heard later on the BBC shortwave service in Malta, New Zealand, Australia, America and Canada.

There were the usual Holiday at Home appearances and in the last concert on September 4th Mr and Mrs Davies celebrated their Silver Wedding anniversary. The Choir presented them with a mirror, a bouquet of roses and an illuminated address. This was signed by all the girls and headed with the opening bars of "Music in my Heart", the Choir's signature tune. Most of the programme consisted of requests from the audience of family and friends and one came in a rather novel way. A note was left on the steering wheel of Mr Davies' car. The Choir sang their new number "Such Lovely Things are These". Originally for an orchestra, Mr Davies had it arranged for the Choir and in one place the Choir were actually singing nine different parts.

Early September saw them in Worthing. The Council there produced an unusual booklet listing the weekly events happening in the town. The Luton Girls Choir programme was in the centre and the booklet could be stuck down round the edges and sent as a postcard to a friend.

At home there was another local broadcast, this time from the Luton Grammar School. Called "First House" it also featured Louis Steven on violin, Ivor Dennis on piano and Augustus Lowe on the organ. The audience were told when they could applaud and for how long, due to time constraints.

The Choir singing at one of the bandstands in Wardown Park, 1950's. Photo Luton News.

At the Watford concert on Sunday September 25th the new souvenir booklet appeared, the profits to go towards the proposed American tour. The earlier souvenir of the Choir was an A3 page folded into a leaflet, with an individual photograph of all the members. The brochure for the tour was a more glossy affair, a small booklet with a picture of Janet Bandy one of the Choir members on the front cover. (John Gibbs gave her a framed copy of this photo, which she still cherishes today.) The centre spread was of the Choir taken while they were singing at the Alma Theatre. Mr Davies at the piano featured on the inside cover and there were small pictures of all the girls with their name and what part they sang. The Trustees, Peggy Coggins, John Gibbs and Mrs Davies were all included and there was a short article on the town itself.

In October when the Luton Savoy cinema celebrated its 11th birthday the Choir sang at the concert, helping to entertain 150 local old people. Thanks to the generosity of the Town's traders the old folk dined free in the cinema cafe and then saw the show. On Wednesday October 19th the Choir sang at a concert for "The Mission to Seamen" at the Kingsway Hall London. Princess Elizabeth had made a generous donation to the charity from the Royal Wedding Presents Fund, the money being used to buy a motor boat for work on the Clyde. The craft was called the Princess Elizabeth and the Youth Section of the organisation had raised money to help cover the cost of its launch. The money was received by the Princess at the rally and as she came onto the platform the Choir sang "Princess Elizabeth of England". After the Princess had spoken on the work of the Mission the Choir sang "Dream of Olwen". They also sang before and after the Princess' appearance. Suitably, the Band appearing with the Choir was that of the Royal Marines, Chatham Group.

Anne Norcross can remember the concert well as she should have been in hospital. She asked her mother to ring and cancel her appointment and after the singing she had tea with the Princess and sat next to Princess Mary the Princess Royal. Much better than hospital and she had a lovely memory to cherish.

From October to December 1949 the Choir took part in a series of 11 broadcasts called "Gala Concert". These also featured Rawicz and Landauer, Anne Ziegler and Webster Booth and Mark Lubbock and his orchestra and were heard live at 8 o'clock each Monday night. Two coaches would leave Luton each Monday; one with the schoolgirls and those leaving work at 5.30pm, departed at 6 o'clock. Taxis picked up the girls leaving work at 6 pm and the second coach left about 6.15 pm.

Packed teas were provided and the first lot of girls were able to rehearse with the soloists and orchestra when they arrived at about 7.15pm. The second coach arrived about 7.45 pm and they were on air at 8 o'clock. Each week there would be two new numbers and the Choir would only have two rehearsals in which to learn the songs.

December 28th saw the Choir again on television appearing for about 14 minutes in another "Music Hall", this time from St Pancras Town Hall. Other stars included Tessie O'Shea, Harry Green, Leon Cortez, Anne Ziegler and Webster Booth. Although it was an evening performance rehearsals started at 11am, meaning that only the schoolgirls and those on holiday could be there. Mr Davies conducted the TV orchestra and possibly due to not having a full Choir rehearsal there was a slight hitch at the beginning of the first number: according to the local press this was not noticed by many people. About 30 Lutonians travelled to see the Choir and appeared in the general audience shots.

America

There had been great excitement when it was announced in June 1949 that the choir would sing in America and Canada. Articles appeared in many papers and magazines, both in the States and in England. In September there was even an article in the "Farmer and Stockbreeder" due to Mr Davies being an agricultural agent. There were the usual rumours and controversy and some heated words when the Americans suggested that the girls be "glamorised" for their tour. Mr Davies responded that "their mothers would decide how glamorous the girls would look with regard to both make up and the "skimpy" look. On stage they would wear long blue dresses and look completely and sweetly British. His girls were singers not strippers".

The tour was arranged for April 1950 and the impresario in charge was Sol Hurok. There was much to arrange at the British end. By March permission had been sought from the Bow Street Court in London for 43 of the younger girls to sing abroad. Sureties of £1000 had been given to the courts and the girls were insured for £1000. £7,100 had been raised towards the travelling costs and arrangements made for the girls to stay with families of members of the Rotary clubs in America and Canada.

Parents had to write a letter giving permission for the girls to travel with the choir and Mr Davies had drawn up a set of rules of behaviour and sent each girl a letter. He had compiled a report on each one taken from comments made by audiences, friends and admirers. Covering stage presentation and discipline as well as the more personal points of disposition, temper, friendliness, cheerfulness, conscientiousness and conversational ability, these reports were private and confidential but he urged the girls to correct any noticeable shortcomings.

The girls went in two groups on Saturday mornings to Yardleys in Bond Street to be shown professionally how to apply stage make up and how to clean their face afterwards. They were each given bags of Yardley goods for use on the tour.

A concert for publicity purposes was arranged at the HMV recording studios and the Choir had to face an audience of British and American news correspondents. In a short programme the girls had to convince the reporters they would make the grade on tour. Traditionally the press never applauded but the American representatives who had just "dropped in" for a few minutes, stayed right through till the end and the last items did receive applause.

There was a break halfway through the evening to allow the journalists to interview the girls for their reactions to the tour. It was the "babes" who attracted the attention and Marion Jones faced a barrage of questions from the New York Herald Tribune reporter.

Many firms gave clothes to the Choir as a means of advertising their wares in America. Charles Butler Ltd. of Nottingham presented the blue Robia voile stage frocks; material was supplied by Tootal Broadhurst and Lee Ltd. and grey jersey and dusty pink Moygashall materials for other dresses.

Mangold of Luton supplied each girl with a tartan skirt and stole and Kosie Knitwear Ltd provided the matching Chitnit sweaters. Seventy smartly cut Mornessa coats were fashioned by Ornstein and Masoff Ltd. from blue velour cloth supplied by James Hare Ltd. and British Bata Shoe Co Ltd. gave two pairs of shoes per girl, blue calf for walking and red doe for stage wear. Fully fashioned stockings were courtesy of Wolsey Ltd.

Luton Knitting Co. Ltd. supplied the maroon berets for casual wear while the Lancashire Felt and Fibre Co. Ltd. donated fur felt navy hoods to be made into hats by the Hats Publicity Association Ltd. Sundry accessories were also provided, Crocdex handbags from Universal Leather Goods of Blackburn, three pairs of gloves each from R and J Pulman Ltd. and Perveil underwear for all the girls from John Beals of Nottingham. Jacqmar Ltd. gave each girl a pale blue scarf with pictures of London landmarks and a border reading Luton Girls Choir USA and Canada 1950. One of theses scarves was later lost overboard on a trip to Belfast and the girls thought if it was ever found people might think they had been shipwrecked on their way to America.

A farewell concert sponsored by Luton Council was arranged at the Alma Theatre on the 2nd of April, ABC Ltd giving free use of both theatre and staff. In Liverpool, there was to be a civic reception on Good Friday April 7th when the choir would be received by the Lord Mayor of Liverpool. This would be followed by a concert in the evening at the Philharmonic Hall. The choir were due to sail on the "Franconia" on the 8th of April.

Then came the awful shock, the tour was off. Girls and parents were summoned to the Town Hall where they were told the devastating news. Not enough concerts had been arranged for them in America and the itinerary that had been sent for them was not true.

Monies raised for the travelling fund were returned but most firms said the girls could keep the clothes; it was thought they had suffered enough disappointment. To repay this kindness the girls had a 10 minute fashion show before their following concerts to display the clothes for the various firms.

The choir also gave a concert at a dinner for the firm of Charles Butler Ltd. and two concerts for Bata's. They spent the day at Bata's where they were given lunch before their afternoon concert. Tea followed and then there was dancing in the social hall till the evening performance. The girls were partnered by students from the Bata Technical College and the music was supplied by the Bata Hotel Trio. There was supper after the evening concert and as the girls had enjoyed the meals very much they insisted on thanking the chef, so a blushing George Ballard was brought from the kitchen to take a bow. As a final gift, Bata gave each of the girls a pair of nylon stockings before they left.

The farewell concert at the Alma went ahead as planned. The Choir sang with the band of the Grenadier Guards and the compere was Ronnie Waldman. A dress show was arranged in the interval by Stones Fashion House of George Street and in the programme notes Mr Davies thanked all the sponsors and donors of gifts and had a message of thanks for the girls, parents and audience. His summing up re the tour was :-"We will be stronger as a result of our disappointing experience and it might be that good will ultimately result".

February 1950 was another busy month with the Choir appearing in the Film Festival on Sunday 5th, rehearsing in the morning and singing in the afternoon. They then gave a concert at Walthamstow in the evening. In the interval Souvenir Brochures were sold to raise funds and one which had been signed by all the girls was auctioned, selling for £3. Marion Jones had spent most of her morning recording her part in "Chapel in the Valley" at the BBC before joining the rest of the girls.

On the 12th, the girls sang at Leicester with the Luton Choral Society. This was the first time the two Choirs had appeared together in a complete concert; the Choral Society appeared in their new style full length blue dresses for the occasion and this grouping became known as a Blue Rhapsody Concert. Enquiries had been received from several other towns and cities for a Blue Rhapsody performance, so Mr Davies watched carefully for audience reaction. Seven coaches left Bridge Street, the Choirs travelling together to sing in the De Montford Hall to an audience of over 3,000 people.

To help soften the blow of the cancelled tour, on May 10th 1950 the 70 girls who should have gone to America were invited by the Lord Mayor of London, Sir Frederick Rowland, to be his guests for tea in the Mansion House. Of course they were asked to "sing for their supper" and they obliged with "Lift up your Hearts", "Charlie is my Darling" and "Count your Blessings". When the girls stepped into the scarlet and blue reception hall they were greeted by the sound of their own music played by the string sextet of the Band of the Grenadier guards. The Band had performed with the Choir many times and the guards' appearance was the idea of Major Harris as a gesture of goodwill to the Choir.

Various Luton dignitaries, as well as Mr and Mrs Davies, were presented to the Lord Mayor; these included the Mayor and Mayoress, Mr and Mrs Sinfield, Mr and Mrs John Gibbs, who was the Honorary publicity man and Mr Alec Webb, who was the Transport Organiser.

After tea the girls were joined by the rest of the Choir to sing in St. Paul's

Cathedral, the concert lasting for 2 hours. Double decker buses conveyed several hundred supporters from Luton and the Choir sang to an audience of 3,500 people, 500 of whom had to stand. People had queued outside before the performance, the queue going right round the building. This was the first time an amateur choir from outside London had ever had the honour to sing in the Cathedral and the proceeds from the concert were shared between the "Lord Mayor's National Thanksgiving Fund" and "Christian Aid".

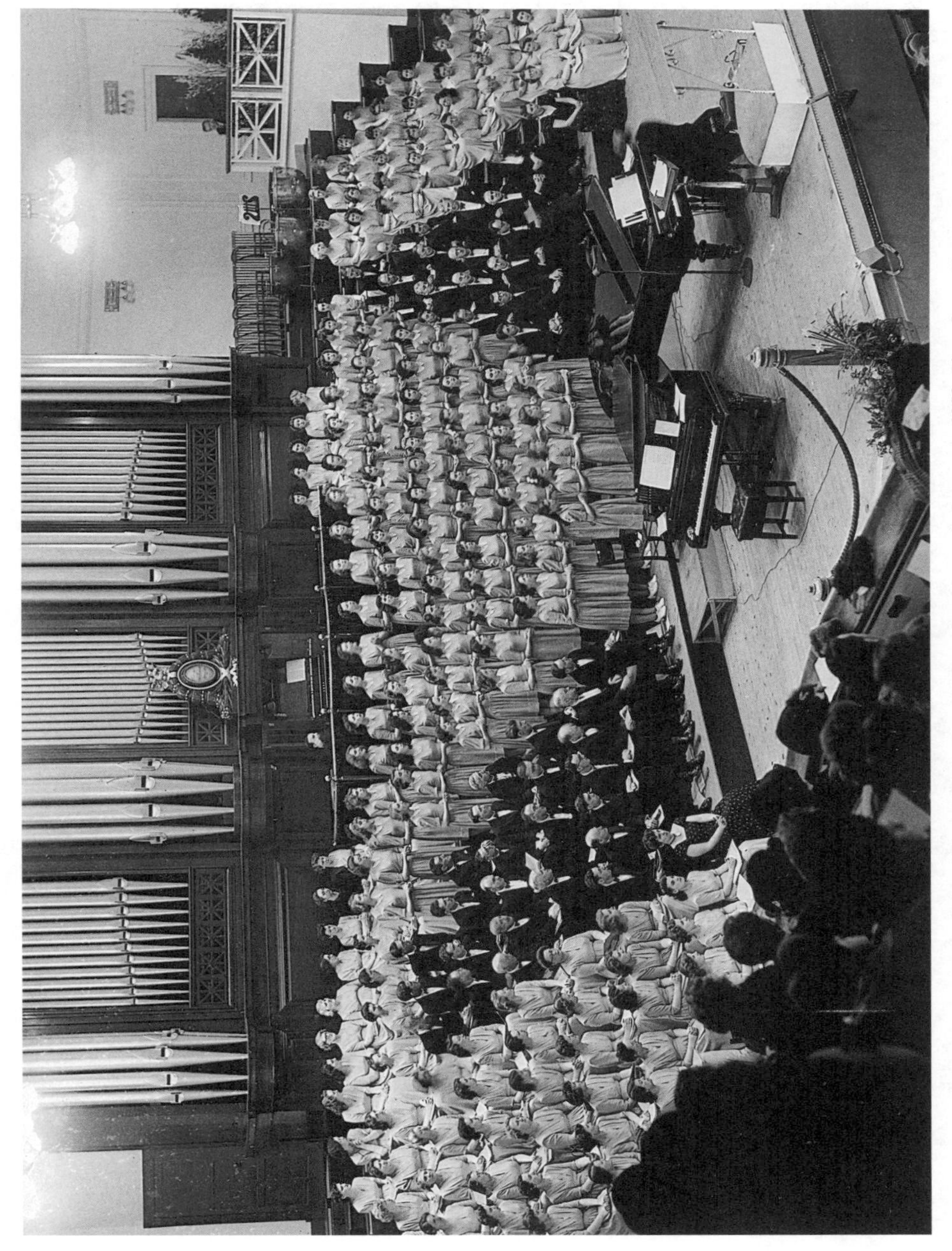

At the De Montford Hall in Leicester, the first Blue Rhapsody Concert in 1950. Photo Luton News.

At the Mansion House with the Lord Mayor of London, Sir Frederick Rowland. Photo Luton News.

"Singing for their supper" at the Mansion House. Photo Luton News.

Chapter Eight

Ireland and the Fifties

In May 1950 the Choir did cross the sea for a tour when on Friday 26th they went to Belfast in Northern Ireland. A party of 92 left Luton at 3.30pm for Heysham Harbour, a train making an unscheduled stop at Luton especially to pick up the Choir. They arrived at the port at 11pm, eight lucky girls who were engaged being allowed to take their fiances with them.

On arrival Mr Davies ordered that the girls should go directly to their cabins "in the interests of her own health and that of her parents". It was a wet weekend and the crossing was quite rough. Mr and Mrs Davies retired to their cabins on the surface deck but most of the Choir were down below. Many of the girls were seasick and the older ones spent the night comforting and cleaning up "the babies" and finding stewards to "mop up". Nobody got much sleep but Mr Davies did not seem to realise why all the girls were tired and drained the next day.

The boat docked at 7am and by 7.45 am. two double decker buses were carrying the girls to breakfast at the Ulster Menu Co Restaurant in Wellington Street. It was then on to the Presbyterian Hostel where they stayed during the weekend, stage dresses being left at the Grosvenor Hall next door.

The Lord Mayor of Belfast, Councillor W.E. Johnston, gave the Choir a Civic reception where the girls sang "Count your Blessings". After lunch it was on to the Grosvenor Hall, first for a rehearsal and then a concert. This unfortunately coincided with the Balmoral Show in Belfast, so they did not have a very large audience. The Belfast Girl Singers entertained the Luton party to tea at the hostel before the evening performance which was again at the Grosvenor Hall. This time the girls sang to a packed house and received one of their greatest concert receptions. The Deputy Lord Mayor asked the Choir to sing "The Lord is my Shepherd" and the audience joined in. As well as soloists the audience were entertained by duets on the piano played by Molly Litchfield and Eileen Gaskin.

On Sunday there was no concert, so the girls went on the 250 mile Portrush circular sightseeing tour. This included the Giant's Causeway, Ballycastle and Carrickfergus and they arrived back at 6pm after a very full day.

On Monday morning the girls toured Belfast and after lunch the Parliament buildings at Stormont were specially opened for them to visit. Their final concert on the Monday evening was again in the Grosvenor Hall. A grand reception from an audience of about 2,000 showed that the singing and piano duets were very much appreciated.

The girls had to leave for home immediately after the concert, having only 30 minutes before their ship sailed and they were escorted to the docks by two trams full of admirers with many people in the streets to wave goodbye. The Belfast Girl Singers were at the docks and the two Choirs sang to each other, the Luton girls singing "Someday we shall Meet Again" and "Now is the Hour" while the Irish girls replied with a northern folk song and "Will you N'er Come Back Again?" They both then joined in singing "Auld Lang Syne". Several friendships were started that weekend and some of the Luton girls revisited Ireland later.

On the boat home the girls were given 2/6 to purchase their supper and the boat docked at Heysham at 5am. Breakfast was in Leeds at the Queen's Hotel before they left by train at 9.43am arriving in Luton at 1.50pm. The tour was commercially sponsored with the fares being paid by the promoter Harold Holt. The choir wore the clothes that had been given to them for the ill fated American tour.

Luckily the concert at the Alma Theatre on Sunday June 4th, with the Choir and the Band of the Royal Marines from Portsmouth, was scheduled as a dual event. It was originally planned to welcome the girls home from the American tour as well as celebrating the 40th anniversary of Skefko Ball Bearing Company, so although there had been no tour, the concert still took place. The Skefko employees could either attend a ball or the concert and 3,200 people chose the concert. Other guests included Dr Charles Hill, who was the M.P. for Luton and also the "Radio Doctor", and the Mayor and Mayoress of Luton, Councillor and Mrs R. Colin Large. As a memento of the occasion all the members of the Choir were presented with a blue hairbrush by Skefko.

The programme for the June appearance at the Luton Bandstand was a hint of things to come with the Gala Rhapsody programmes in later years. Mr Davies organised a Yesterday, Today and Tomorrow concert with 80 current members, 30 ex members and 30 future singers. All of them sang but at this time they did not perform together.

Their trip to Eastbourne on Sunday July 6th 1950 was quite an endurance for many people that day. Margaret Hill missed the coach which was taking the girls to Eastbourne. Waiting at Kingsway until she realised she had her arrangements wrong, she then hitch hiked and caught buses to Barnet, took the tube to Charing Cross and then Victoria Station and reached Eastbourne in time for rehearsals. The Choir were singing with the Luton Choral Society in a Blue Rhapsody Concert and there were 200 people on the stage. This proved too warm for two of the cast who fainted. 500 people of the 1,300 in the audience had queued in the hot sun for their tickets and the show was a lengthy one, the interval coming when most programmes would have finished. A hectic tiring day for a lot of people.

The Bank Holiday, August 26th and 27th saw the Choir in Wales again, this time as guests of the Aberystwyth YMCA at their Mid Wales Eisteddfod. On the Saturday night the Choir sang in the King's Hall to a full house even though 11,000 people were elsewhere attending the Eisteddfod finals.

After the performance as usual the choir members stayed with various hosts. Two girls were given a door key and the address of their digs for the night. They found their own way to the house, ate the supper which had been left for them and went to bed praying they were in the right house. They did not meet their hosts until the following day!

On the Sunday the girls sang in a marquee in a field where, in spite of a cloudburst and the field being swamped with water, there was an audience of 7,000 with a further 2,000 listening outside. The Choir thought people would not attend because of the weather but the Welsh officials described it as a mere shower. The audience joined in as soloist Marion Jones was singing a Welsh folk tune and there was a great climax when everybody sang the "Hallelujah Chorus". Other singers on the programme were Walter Midgley, a tenor from the Royal Opera House and Jennifer Vyvyan a soprano, the solo pianist and accompanist being Charles Clements.

Twenty six stewards were available to help in the marquee and to sell Souvenir Booklets of the Choir. A van and two cars were put at the Choir's disposal to "fetch and carry" and when the girls were off duty they enjoyed a steamer trip and the company of an off duty policeman who went along with them to take pictures. The shop windows were full of Choir records and photos of its members and the girls were often surrounded by autograph hunters.

Mr Davies even found time to take two of the Choir members to visit one of their great fans, an elderly lady of 80 years, who had followed the Choir since it began. Her son was Councillor Griffiths of Aberystwyth and he was so impressed by the kindness of the visit that he wrote to the Luton News to tell them.

In September Brian Johnston was in Margate to produce two concerts to be broadcast for Variety Concert Hall on the Light Programme, one on Sunday and one on Monday. The Choir appeared in the Sunday one which was recorded in the afternoon, 2,000 people queuing for the performance in the Winter Gardens. Appearing in the same show were comedian Terry O'Neill, the Petersen Brothers who played the guitar and the Arthur Knight Quintet. After the broadcast Brian Johnston asked the Choir to sing his favourite tune, "We'll Gather Lilacs", they also sang "Charlie is my Darling" for him.

In the evening another audience of 2,000 were at the Choir's second performance, 500 people queuing for the unreserved seats. Mr Davies's new song "My Heart is Singing" made its first public appearance: it was announced by Pamela Smith and was received with great enthusiasm. Mr Davies did some customer surveying when he asked the audience how many of them were hearing the Choir live for the first time; there were about 1,750 people.

Two weeks later, on September 17th, the Choir were appearing at Worthing Pier Pavilion as part of the town's Municipal Diamond Jubilee Celebrations. A double spread coloured photograph of the Choir featured in the programme.

When the Choir were in Worthing it became their custom to have lunch at the Dinner Gong Restaurant and over the years they received several cakes specially prepared for them. This time they were presented with a cake decorated in scarlet and blue with the Choir's symbol of music on it, together with "Welcome to Worthing". The cake later went on show in Luton at the Electricity Showrooms before being cut up and shared amongst the Choir. In the evening before the concert the Choir were entertained to tea in the Town Hall.

Guests to the sell out concert included the Lord and Lady Mayor and Mayoress of London and the Choir pianists Mollie Litchfield and Eileen Gaskin had the honour of being presented to them both as well as to the Mayor and Mayoress of Worthing.

October 1950 saw two appearances by the Choir at the Empress Hall in London. On the 15th there was a Scarlet and Blue concert, the first to be performed in London. Mr Davies felt Londoners would support them after the success of the St Paul's Cathedral concert and he was right, the Choir, wearing their Robia voile blue dresses, singing to a packed house. 10 double decker buses carried nearly 500 people from Luton to the concert for a successful evening. Their supporters were thrilled that Luton girls could fill such a large venue.

On the 20th October they were back again at the Hall. Over the years the Choir sang at several of the El Alamein Reunions and at the 5th one they were there with the Band of the Coldstream Guards. Other military musicians included the trumpeters and string orchestra of the Royal Artillery Mounted Band and the Band of the Royal Marines, Plymouth. The community singing was led by Ralph Reader.

That year a 13 foot stained glass window, dedicated to the 8th Army, was being installed in the Lady Chapel of Cairo Cathedral. It had been on display in the Victoria and Albert Museum and was brought to the Empress Hall for the reunion as the feature of that year's pageant, entitled "The Spirit was Unbroken". The window was seen by a British family visiting the Cathedral and they reflected on past great battles leading up to El Alamein. The story was narrated by Lionel Gamlin and starred Jack Hawkins as the father, John Howard Davis as the son and Elizabeth Allen as the mother.

Also taking part in the evening were Vera Lynn, Richard Murdoch and Michael Bentine. There were many speeches including one by the hero of the battle, Field Marshall The Viscount Montgomery of Alamein KG. GCB. DSO. and also by the Right Honourable Winston Churchill OM. CH. MP. President Eisenhower and his wife were at the reunion and three lucky members of the Choir were introduced to them after the show by Mr Davies. Field Marshall Montgomery remarked to Mr Davies "What a pretty looking lot of girls, where ever do you find them?"

During that year the Choir had made 24 broadcasts, 4 of them in September, and they were one of the most popular requests on Housewife's Choice.

Mr Davies did enjoy meeting famous people and in February 1951 when the Choir were singing at Drury Lane he and his wife were presented to the Prime Minister, Mr Attlee at the All Star Variety Concert. This was sponsored by the Hendon Labour Party for the Barbara Ayrton-Gould Memorial. As an MP she had championed the cause of the "unwanted child" and had also organised the relief committee for miners' wives and families during the 1926 lockout.

Many artistes supported the concert including Dame Sybil Thorndike, Harriet Cohen, Peter Cavanagh and Carroll Levis and his discoveries. It was a busy night for the Choir; they sang for 15 minutes in the first half and were then taken by coach, still in their blue dresses and red shoes, to give a two hour concert at Islington Town Hall.

In the 50's there was a change of venue at Easter and for several years it was Cornwall. From March 23rd - 27th 1951 it was the people of Truro and district who enjoyed listening to the Choir. The trip was arranged by the social committee of Holman Bros. Ltd., an engineering firm in Camborne. Negotiations had started three years previously and various difficulties had to be overcome. Mr Davies himself visited Cornwall to supervise arrangements. Venues with a large enough capacity to offset expenses had to be found, catering details needed sorting and accommodation was required for 80 people.

When the Choir arrived on the Friday they were given supper and introduced to their sponsors and respective hosts who would be providing accommodation for the weekend. There were two concerts in Truro on the Saturday, one in the afternoon and one in the evening. On Sunday the girls were able to enjoy the Cornish countryside during a sightseeing trip to St Ives and Land's End before being entertained to tea by the Mayor and Mayoress of Penzance. The evening concert at the Ritz Cinema in Penzance was the first in the town's Festival of Britain celebrations.

St Mary's Methodist Church congregation were involved with accommodating the Choir which featured in a long article in the Church magazine, together with details of contributions and support from the congregation and local people. Apart from donations of money they provided 32 chickens, lcwt of potatoes, 50 cauliflowers, butter and eggs. Meals were served in the dining room of the Truro Public School where local people also worked in the kitchens and looked after the tables. On the Saturday evening the community effort was also generously supported by the Deputy Mayor and friends of the Church.

To commemorate the tour Mrs Davies was given a painting of a Cornish coastal scene and when the girls left to return to Luton they were each given sheaves of fresh daffodils; many of the hosts said it was a pleasure to entertain the young ladies.

The tour certainly stuck in the memory of Joan Folks. Joan and her friend were collected by a farmer driving a clapped out estate car, no suspension and with sheep in the boot area. They stayed at a lovely old farm house, in a pretty bedroom but it had a commode in the corner. The girls said they would prefer to use the toilet so were escorted down the field to a shack containing a wooden seat over a ditch. There were brambles all round and spiders for company.

In the evening after the concert, the coach did a main road tour taking the girls back to their digs. The name of the farm was called and the two girls got off. They watched as the lights of the coach disappeared; it was 11 o'clock at night, pitch dark and they were alone! They could not find the farm gate and the night was full of horrible groans and noises. Joan doesn't know how they got through the field full of cowpats and back to the cottage. The farmer was most amused by their experiences but he did lend them a torch for the next night. The "Townees" were not used to living without their "mod cons". Joan did keep in touch with the farmer and later visited him while she was on holiday in Cornwall.

Whitsun of that year found the Choir first in London and then in Blackpool. On Saturday the 12th they were broadcasting in the Festival of Britain "London Rhapsody" series. Accommodation could not be found overnight for the Choir so it was back to Luton and then up at the crack of dawn, back on the coach and back to London, this time to catch the "Royal Scot" train to Blackpool where they were doing two concerts for Harry Fielding Productions, one at 6.20pm and one at 8.15pm. It was every organiser's nightmare; the train was 75 minutes late and the girls did not reach the stage until 5.30pm. In half an hour Mr Davies had re-draped the backcloth, "sized" the girls and rehearsed them for a 45 minute performance. They had a meal at 6pm and the doors opened only 10 minutes late. There were other artistes in the concert, the choir singing for most of the second half of the programme.

The girls did have time to enjoy some of the delights of Blackpool and were special guests at the circus. They received warm applause from the audience when they were announced and picked out of the crowd by spotlight.

One of the girls can remember sharing a room with two others in the same hotel as Mr and Mrs Davies. She was not very popular when she woke the guests with her nightmare.

The Royal Festival Hall opened in 1951 and the Choir appeared in a memorable concert on the night of July 7th. With Tom Jenkins and his Palm Court Orchestra, Bram Gay on the trumpet and Reginald Foort at the organ, they sang to an audience of 8,000. As well as the evening performance they sang on two afternoons attracting more people than any other afternoon concert.

Prior to the evening performance, Mr John Gibbs and two members of the Choir were interviewed in the festival Telekinema and it was relayed to the audience in the hall. 560 local people went to support their Choir and many travelled to the Festival Hall on a specially chartered double decker bus. The Mayor and Mayoress and members of the Luton Council were there and the Choir's Trust gave a reception; guests included the Vice Chairman of London County Council and his wife and the Mayor and Mayoress of Lambeth.

The girls were delighted with the spacious dressing rooms in the Festival Hall, with mirrors and places to hang up their new Festival dresses which they were wearing for the first time. They even had seats and the stage was a joy to perform on. It was all a far cry from the pokey little church halls where they often appeared.

The girls continued their concerts as usual with appearances at the seaside. At Worthing in September they again had lunch at the Dinner Gong Restaurant and received a cake specially baked for them. This time it was surmounted by a model theatre showing the girls in their blue dresses, being conducted by Mr Davies at the piano. The people of Luton admired it later when it went on display in the Gas Showroom's window.

During the later part of the year there were lots of uniforms involved. In October at the Empress Hall in Earls Court the girls again sang at the El Alamein reunion on the 19th, Winston Churchill, Lord Montgomery and General Eisenhower being amongst an appreciative audience. On the 27th there were 10 admirals amongst the sailors listening to the Choir and the Massed Bands of HM Royal Marines, Portsmouth, during the Royal Naval Association's Reunion at the Royal Festival Hall.

On November 11th a section of the Choir, together with the Luton Choral Society and the London Philharmonic Orchestra provided the music at the Remembrance Day Concert in Watford Town Hall.

Uniforms of a different sort were in evidence when the Choir sang at the Granada Cinema in Kettering on Sunday November 25th. The concert was in aid of the Fire Services National Benevolent Fund and all 2,000 seats were full. Some standing was allowed but many people were turned away. There was a brief reunion when a former member of the Choir, Mrs K. Saunders, then living in Kettering, joined Mr Davies on the stage for a chat. The girls made good use of the Market Street Fire Station, as part of it was converted into a dressing room for them to change into their blue dresses.

On Friday 7th December the Choir appeared on Television for the third time, the previous Monday being spent in rehearsals at the Central Mission in Luton. Mr Davies had formed a TV section of girls grouped into a picture, some standing, some sitting and said he would monitor audience reaction to the new grouping. As their contribution the Choir sang a selection from Walt Disney's "Bambi" and an Ivor Novello song, the finale being "Lullaby of Broadway".

By the end of that year the Choir had made 31 broadcasts and their fees for a 30 minute slot on radio for one of their broadcasts was 15 guineas. They were giving

50 concerts a year away from the district and at least 8 requests were being made to the office each day so choices had to be made.

In January 1952 the Choir made a special tape recording for one of their New Zealand fans. Mr William Sexton had corresponded with Mrs Gladys West of Luton for 40 years, originally making contact when he answered a note put in the band of a hat exported to New Zealand. He had been a junior assistant in a store in Palmerstone North and she had been a "finisher" in the hat trade in Luton. Mr Sexton was asked by the New Zealand Broadcasting station to do a series on the Choir, so they made the tape and the Mayor, Councillor R Colin Large also added a few words. The tape was played in New Zealand on the last programme of the series.

In February a Festival of British Radio was staged in the Royal Albert Hall. Harold Fielding had been asked to find programmes to fill the Hall on ten consecutive nights from 31st January to the 9th February. Calling on his experience of finding stars for the "Music for the Millions" seaside concerts, he decided to give British performers a chance. The Choir and the Band of the Irish Guards with the pianists Rawicz and Landauer filled the Saturday slot. Two coach loads of "fans" went to hear them and the girls were on stage for two and a half hours without a break. Two of the girls can remember being taken to task by Mr Davies due to members of the Irish Guards making them giggle during the performance of the famous pianists.

The demands of the weekend March 1st and 2nd caused even Mr Davies some trepidation. The Choir were due to appear at a Blue Rhapsody concert on Saturday at the Royal Festival Hall and the Daily Mail National Radio Awards ceremony on Sunday at the London Coliseum. On the proceeding Thursday they had a performance at Battersea Town Hall and a rehearsal on the Friday for the weekend activities. Much thought went into the arrangements. The girls were instructed to be prompt to enable the coach to leave Luton at 6pm on Thursday. The journey was six miles longer than their normal London run and there were no motorways in the early '50s, so evening travel took a long time. The Friday night rehearsal at Youth Headquarters was from 6.30pm - 8.30pm so that the girls would not be tired for Saturday. Girls at work were allowed 1/- per head for tea to avoid them having to go home first.

The following letter was sent to each girl and the two days organised with military precision.

Dear Member,

As a result of developments in connection with our immediate activities during the coming days, I thought it wise to formulate an itinerary so as to avoid confusion in my attempt to meet particularly the new "programme" demands made by the BBC

"Radio Award" producers of both Television and Sound.

Some few days ago I nearly had a heart attack when they said they required us in two numbers which were not in our repertoire and consequently the whole of Monday last was given over to securing the necessary musical arrangements for that purpose. Both arrangers and copyists are working almost through the night in order that I might have the copies by Friday and this will be the toughest "nut" we jointly have yet to crack, particularly with the Royal Festival Hall concert on our heels as it were.

Naturally I have thought and thought again on just how to overcome such a situation. On Monday I even sought release from the programme but the BBC say the public demand our appearance and that such a step would be breaking faith with all concerned. As they put it, this is the result of " fame" and that we must use every endeavour to meet the situation.

In attaching hereto, therefore, the particulars of an S.O.S. itinerary, I seek your whole-hearted co-operation in endeavouring to carry it out. If, as I believe, the Choir has in the past meant anything to you, your conscientious reaction will mean you will show that sacrifice which will assure a successful end.

In this respect I am making no personal appeal but leave it to you to so plan your next few days as will enable you to assist without prejudice in overcoming the desperate situation in a conscientious manner. I am going to thank you in anticipation and leave it at that. With kind regards and best wishes for your enjoyment of these thrilling experiences.

Yours Sincerely, Arthur E Davies.

On the Saturday morning the Television section (except for the 5 girls who were working in the morning) left Alma Street at llam. The coach went directly to the Cora Hotel where rooms for the night were allocated, the TV dresses hung up and the shoes and mittens stowed away. On to the Strand Corner House for lunch at 1.15pm, each girl taking her Festival dress, red shoes and a coat hanger. (Yes even this was specified).

The full Choir, plus the other five girls, were to leave Alma Street at 12.45pm; late comers would be left behind. The full Choir had to take their dresses, shoes and a coat hanger and be seated in the stalls of the Festival Hall at 2.45pm ready for "placing" on stage with the Choral Society. After the rehearsal, Peggy Coggins handed out tea tickets.

With so many performers, stewards were needed behind the scenes to guide people through the complex arrangements of doors at different levels, leading to the stage.

The concert in the evening was a "Blue Rhapsody" compered by McDonald Hobley, the Choir singing with the Luton Choral Society and the Band of the Irish Guards.

There were 3,000 in the audience, 280 standing and as the Luton News correspondent could not get a ticket he had to hear the concert in the listening room.

He wrote about this unusual happening. Mr Davies had a cold to add to his concerns about the week's activities and it may have been this as a cumulation of things to worry about that made him mislay his music. As he was looking for the next piece he held the Choir on the last note of the song. McDonald Hobley coming on to announce the next number realised they had not finished and conferred with Lieutenant Jaeger. The audience laughed and when they stopped, the choir were still holding the note. The applause meter went over the top as the audience gave the highest acclaim for showmanship, stage management and control of breath from the singing point of view.

Augustus Lowe, at the Festival organ, played the "Solemn Melody" in memory of George VI and there was a tribute to Queen Elizabeth from the full ensemble. This was the third "Blue Rhapsody" where the Choir, the Choral Society and a Band performed together and Corporal R.Oades who was a solo trumpeter later featured prominently in the life of one of the Choir.

The Daily Mail National Radio Awards was at the Coliseum on the Sunday. This was the second time the awards had been presented and the programme was in two halves, the TV awards being televised and the radio awards broadcast on the BBC Light programme. The Choir featured in both parts. They were actually listed amongst the top ten finalists for the Radio Award that year.

The TV unit left the Cora hotel at 10.45am on Sunday morning for a rehearsal at the Coliseum, had lunch at the Strand Corner House and then returned to the Coliseum for a "sound" rehearsal. They met up with the rest of the Choir who had left Alma Street at lpm. Tea for all after the rehearsal was again at the Strand Corner House and then it was back to the Coliseum for the actual performance.

Wilfred Pickles was the Radio Personality of the Year; the best programme was "Take It From Here". TV Personality was Richard Dimbleby and "What's My Line?" the best TV programme. Other stars at the awards ceremonies were Dick Bentley, Jimmy Edwards and Ben Lyons with Bebe Daniels.

After all this the girls were back at work or school on the Monday.

The end of March also caused difficulties when the Choir went to Brighton to sing in the Dome. They left Luton by coach on Saturday at 12.30pm and after a snowy journey they got as far as Victoria station in London. As the weather reports said that the snow was falling at a rate of 2 inches per hour, it was obviously unwise to continue by road. Mr Davies spoke to the station master who issued a bulk ticket for the 75 members of the party to allow them to finish their journey by train, the coaches even being allowed on to the platform of the Brighton train to unload the luggage. Leaving Victoria at 4pm. they were collected by coach from Brighton station arriving at their destination one and a half hours late. The Mayor of Brighton had hot soup and tea waiting for them and Mr Davies joked later about singing with a full stomach.

On Sunday after lunch with the Mayor and Mayoress of Hove, the girls were ferried back to the station. Their coaches met them at Victoria and took them safely back to Luton. This was the first time the weather had caused them to abandon their usual form of transport.

Easter 1952 was again spent in Cornwall. 75 members of the Choir together with parents and boyfriends stayed in hotels in St. Ives. Holman Bros. of Camborne were again involved but it was the Methodist Churches of St Austell and Redruth who provided venues for three of the concerts. The Choir, travelling by coach, left Alma Street at 8.00am and reached St. Ives about 9.45pm, a long day.

There were two concerts in St Austell on Saturday, one in the afternoon, the other in the evening. Both were in St John's Church and over 3,000 people, a quarter of the town's population, came to listen to the Choir; people began to queue for the second concert before the first one had finished.

On Sunday the Choir sang at Penzance giving two performances in the Ritz Cinema after their civic reception by the Mayor and Mayoress. At one of the concerts the audience was over 1,000 and afterwards the Choir left by the side door to avoid the crowds who were besieging the main entrance. The programme listed the Choir's repertoire to date and said items for the concert would be chosen from the list.

There was just one performance on Easter Monday, in the evening at Redruth.

Three of the girls, Jeanne Rutty, Estelle Potter and Betty Bird were singing in their last concert before retiring and they duly received their clocks. The people of Cornwall presented Mrs Davies with a hand painted picture and on Tuesday when they left for the long journey home, all the girls were again given bunches of daffodils.

Holman's Social Committee made a profit of £100 which went to help children with tuberculosis. Ten soloists sang during the three days and the commere was Pamela Smith.

Letters later appeared in the Luton News complimenting Mr Davies and Peggy Coggins on the admirable arrangements for the tour and saying how everything had gone so smoothly. Mrs Davies was also praised for her duties as chaperone.

A flashback memory from this tour comes from one of a group of girls staying in a hotel which had a curved wooden staircase leading down to the hall. One girl enjoyed a slide down the banister and landed in a heap amongst a group of her friends at the bottom.

A fortnight later the Choir were singing in Reading at the Palace Theatre. The concert was organised by the Reading area of the National Federation of Old Age Pensioners Association. Not content with just an audience in the theatre, Jim Butcher, the Chairman, made arrangements with the Post Office for the concert to be relayed to three hospitals in the area. Patients in the Royal Berkshire, Battle and Wokingham Hospitals all enjoyed listening to the Choir and then were able to meet the girls when they toured the wards after the show.

A lady of 94 had requested that the Choir sing "Jesu Lover of my Soul" and later she was able to present Mr Davies with a tin of biscuits for the Choir and a hydrangea for his wife. At Woking an old gent of 104 complained that he did not know the tune they had sung for her request, so the Choir gave him an impromptu rendering of the hymn using the tune he liked.

Whitsun that year saw the Choir in Yorkshire with a visit to Scarborough. They were part of Harry Fielding's "Music for the Millions" and gave two concerts in the Floral Hall, one on Saturday, the other on Sunday. As usual there were full houses both times, with people not being able to get seats on the Sunday.

There was a new feature in these concerts. Mr Davies had formed a recording section and with Marion Jones as soloist they sang songs recently recorded by the Choir. Following the tradition of presenting a gift to "birthday girls" if the anniversary fell on the day of a concert, Mrs Davies was given a powder compact from the Choir.

The holiday appearance at Luton Bandstand on June 29th that year took the form of a documentary. The compere was John Gibbs and he told how a girl joins the Choir, how she attends an audition, becomes a member and eventually sings her first solo. During the performance one applicant was actually given an audition and Rita Sygrove sang her first solo.

The Choir Trustees, Stuart Broughall, Ald. G.F. Seaward and Ald. R. Colin Large were introduced along with secretary Peggy Coggins and typist Patricia Corley. Unfortunately the Chairman Mr Rex Parrott was unwell and not able to attend the show.

Mr Gibbs then explained how they organised the Choir's travelling, feeding while away, presentation and clothes, also about the annual X-Ray examination. Two girls who had come to the end of their time with the Choir received their 8 day clocks.

In July the Choir made a week's tour of the North West of England. On Saturday 27th wearing new light navy blue blazers the girls and 36 friends and relatives set off for Blackpool, their first concert being in the famous Opera House. Moving on they sang each night to packed houses in Llandudno and at one concert after five encores Mr Davies had to remind the audience that there was another show that evening. Another time the police had to link arms to make a gangway for the girls to get to their coach, the sort of reception reserved for pop idols of today.

The concerts were again part of Harry Fielding's "Music for the Millions" and in one of his tributes to the Choir in "John Bull" March 29th 1952 he said "Usually when the word "amateur" is mentioned, we expect chaos. From Davies we get quicker service than from many professionals. The girls don't fuss in their dressing rooms. They go on like troopers immaculately dressed and groomed. The standard of singing is incredibly high". This time the Choir sang in the first half of the programme, with Elsie and Doris Waters, George Meaton and Lionel Bowman from South Africa performing in the second half.

Two of the girls were courting members of the Irish Guards, their fellow performers in the "Scarlet and Blue" Concerts. One of the Guards, Bob Oades was on leave at the time and as this coincided with his girl being away, Mr Davies suggested that he accompanied the Choir on their tour. He was able to play the Trumpet Voluntary as the opening number at the concerts.

Six of the girls had "digs" in a lovely old house on the Orme and a visit to the top for the whole Choir was a must. They also managed to visit Betws-y-coed and Conway Castle. The Choir moved on to Rhyl on the Sunday giving two concerts there before returning to Luton on the Monday.

At the end of August the Choir was again asked by the YMCA to sing in the Aberystwyth Eisteddfod, at the Kings Hall on the Saturday and in a marquee on the next day. During the Sunday rehearsal, the Choir faced competition from a robin sitting on one of the ventilators and singing her heart out. During the evening she moved to one of the loudspeakers but decided to let the girls do the singing and sat listening throughout the concert, moving her head from side to side. The audience and Choir were much amused.

At this time such was the Choir's popularity, that although they only stopped for lunch in the town of Worcester on their journey to Aberystwyth, there was a large article and a photograph in the local paper.

1952 was the time of the dreadful floods in Lynmouth and Lynton and the Choir were among the thousands who wanted to help. In September a concert at Watford was arranged within two weeks, with the support of the Watford Town Clerk, the Mayor and the Council. McDonald Hobley, an old friend of the Choir, was away on holiday but wired his willingness to act as compere for the performance and local firms from Watford and Luton covered the cost of the programmes with advertisements. The Mayors of both towns made appeals for money during the interval and the concert raised £200.2s.

As well as charity performances the Choir sang commercially and in September the Machine Tools Traders Association arranged a "Scarlet and Blue" concert at the Festival Hall in conjunction with their trade exhibition at Olympia. In October it was back to the Hall again for a concert to celebrate the 80th birthday of Ralph Vaughan Williams. All the works performed were by him and the Choir sang the children's chorus in "A Song of Thanksgiving". The soloist was Margaret Ritchie and the narrator was Emlyn Williams. Their third visit in quick succession was for the Timber Trades Concert in aid of their Benevolent Society. Many famous broadcasting personalities took part and the Choir presented a "Music you Know and Love" programme with the Irish Guards.

The Choir also paid a second visit that year to Lancashire and Yorkshire in October. They left Luton at 8.15am on the Saturday, lunched in Lichfield and arrived in Manchester at 3.30pm. Their "Scarlet and Blue" Concert with the Irish Guards was at the new Free Trade Hall that evening. The girls enjoyed a night in one of Manchester's largest hotels before moving on to Halifax the following morning. Here the concert was sponsored by the League of Friends of the Halifax Hospital whose secretary had started negotiations in 1951 to try to get the Choir to sing for her cause. It would have been too far and too costly for the Choir to travel just to Halifax for the one concert but at last it was possible to link it with a performance in Manchester and the people of Halifax were able to enjoy the singing and know that their hospital was benefiting as well. Mr Davies had to turn down the requests for encores as conditions on the roads were not very good and he was aware that the Choir had a long way to travel. They arrived home a lot later than expected.

1953 was "Coronation Year" and towns up and down the country celebrated in their own way.

On May 30th the Choir sang in a "live" broadcast from Shepherd's Bush. It was a special celebration concert and they were told the young Queen would be watching. This news was perhaps what helped them later on.

The T.V. Toppers supplied the dance routines and the girls shared a dressing room with them; arriving early at the studios meant the girls were able to bag the best places. The Choir were to sing "Rose of England" the solo to be sung by Victoria Campbell, an opera star of the day. The set was an impressive mock up of the battlements of Windsor Castle, the girls arranged according to size with the star at the highest point. She was to remain hidden until it was time for her to sing. Part of the set was hinged so that when it folded down it would form a Tudor rose and reveal the singer.

In the morning after the girls had been shown their places they were given a time slot for rehearsal and then all trooped off for lunch. On their return they were able to watch the technical rehearsals, sitting just behind the famous names in the show. These included the Lyon family, Bebe, Ben and their children, with Arthur Askey, Terry Thomas and Norman Wisdom. Mr Davies was called away in the afternoon so the Choir were unable to rehearse; this was unfortunate.

When the show went on air the girls were lining the stairs backstage and moved to their places while Norman Wisdom was performing. On cue they duly sang the first two verses of their song then there was a loud "clonk" followed by furtive shuffling. This was one show where the amateurs showed real professional control; the girls were all well trained to carry on regardless so they kept their eyes firmly to the front. The star, instead of giving a powerful rendering, quavered weakly, barely able to hold the tune and devoid of any lyric. The band played on, the Choir watched Mr Davies's face showing various emotions until he could bring them in to sing the last two verses. On leaving the stage they rushed to the dressing room to find Mrs Davies bathing the head of their tallest mezzo soprano, Margaret Matthews. She had been hit on the head as the set unfolded. Margaret said it took all her self control not to squeal like a stuck pig. The star had been more unnerved and later left the theatre in a hurry. After all this excitement it was on to Worthing to appear on Sunday at the Pier Pavilion as part of the town's Coronation Celebrations.

Luton's contribution to 1953 was to stage the pageant "Merrie England" by Edward German. In April 1952 Mr Davies had asked Major General Sir Harold Wernher if he would lend the grounds of Luton Hoo as a theatre. Sir Harold agreed and the town Council took up the idea. Janet King was appointed Organising Secretary and 11 firms guaranteed sponsorship for £10,000 of the £18,000 needed.

The pageant was followed by a cavalcade of the two Elizabethan eras; the setting represented Old Windsor with a reproduction of the castle in the background. Some characters were on horseback and all were in Elizabethan costume, the main body of singers in the chorus of ladies being dressed in loose tunic top smocks with a battlement hemline just below the waist.

All the local singing groups were represented including of course the Luton Girls Choir and the Luton Choral Society. Often mothers would be singing in one group and their daughters in another. There were over 1,000 performers including the Band of the Irish Guards. Seven of the cast were professional, Ann Ziegler and Webster Booth, Nancy Evans, Redvers Llewellyn, Betty Sagon, Graham Clifford and Geoffrey de Lantour. One local star, Amanda Rolfe, played the May Queen and Patricia Corley, a member of the Choir, played Kate. The producer was Harry Powell Lloyd of the Old Vic and Sadlers Wells. He travelled each time from his home in Kensington for the rehearsals which were held in the canteens of Vauxhall Motors and Skefko Ball Bearing Co. Ltd and in the Central Mission Hall, and was very impressed with the overall standard of the cast's singing, dancing and acting. The Irish Guards Band was seated on a floating platform and Major Jaeger swore it was Arthur Davies who pushed him in the lake during the dress rehearsal.

The production took place on an island with the audience seated on the bank opposite. Queen Elizabeth Ist arrived on a barge coming up the lake, accompanied by her two pages, Sheila Land and Sheila Golding, both members of the Choir. Each night two swans would escort the barge as it glided on the lake, which was unscripted but added a nice touch to the arrival.

During the week of the show the girls were picked up from work and taken to the Hoo. Coaches ran from Park Square to the Hoo from 6pm in the evenings and 1.30pm on Saturday to ferry the cast to the stage. Afterwards the coaches took them from the Hoo to as near home as possible, names and addresses having been given in beforehand.

That week the weather was appalling but there were large audiences every night. On the Wednesday evening Sir Harold and Lady Zia Wernher took their house guests including Douglas Fairbanks to the performance.

1953 saw a national recognition and appreciation of Mr Davies's work when he was awarded the MBE in the Coronation Honours List.

From July 30th to August 1st the Choir were once more in Llandudno, appearing in another Harry Fielding presentation. The first half of the programme featured Margo Henderson, the Ballet Montparnasse, Sam Kemp and Jon Pertwee; the Choir sang for most of the second part of the show. The girls were surprised to find that Jon Pertwee's "digs" was his caravan on the pier next to the theatre.

Chapter Nine

A Trip to Denmark: The Parents and Supporters Association

A Trip to Denmark

It was actually in Coronation year that the Choir managed to make their first tour abroad. Initiated by Councillor Skelton during his term as Mayor of Luton the previous year, the choir were to be the guests of the Copenhagen University "Studenter Sangforeningen" or Students of Song, an all male choir which had visited Luton in July 1952.

This was when the Parents and Supporters Group came into being. Formed to help raise money for the Danish trip, it continued to help the Choir with fund raising until the Choir was disbanded. Their first effort was a "Spring Fair" at the Drill Hall in Old Bedford Rd. There was only a year to plan the ten day tour. August was chosen as the best month for the girls to go, being both holiday time in England and the month when they did not give many concerts.

Mr Davies and Peggy Coggins did most of the booking and arrangements, Peggy also checked the dresses while the Music Librarian, Anne Norcross, took charge of the music. Jill Taylor went to London for lessons in Danish as she was both to introduce some of the items and respond to their hosts in their own language. A booklet was produced with the English words of the songs to be sung but the Choir had to learn two songs in Danish, though they found the pronunciation quite difficult.

On the Tuesday morning August 25th, three coaches toured Luton picking up the 76 girls and taking them to the meeting place at Stopsley Green. The Choir were accompanied by the Mayor of Luton, Ald. H.C. Janes and Councillor T. Skelton and their wives. With luggage and girls reorganised the coaches travelled to Colchester where they were met by a former Luton Mayor, Alderman H.C. Hucklesby. He had arranged lunch for the party and he then accompanied them as far as Harwich where they boarded the Kronprinsesse Ingrid.

The ship left England on Tuesday evening. Some of the girls had cabins but most were down below on "Tween Deck" which was uncomfortable, terribly hot and noisy, being next to the engine room. Dinner was a traditional meal of Smorgasbord - (the Danish open sandwich) which did not help and many of the girls were sick, spending time hanging over the side of the boat. There was only Peggy and one other girl at breakfast the following day.

Docking at Esbjerg on the Wednesday morning the choir went by train to Copenhagen, arriving at the headquarters of the Studenter Sangforeningen at about 7pm. Their hosts collected the girls and entertained them for the evening. One girl

On board the ship going to Denmark. Photo Luton News.

Some of the Luton party with the Lord Mayor of London outside Tuborg's Brewery in Denmark.
Photo Luton News.

had been writing to a pen pal for 2/3 years and was able to meet her and stay with her family and Jill Taylor was with a family living only two minutes away from the Tivoli Gardens; she went sight seeing there until midnight.

On Thursday there was an 11 o'clock reception at the Copenhagen Town Hall followed by a sight seeing tour culminating at the Tuborg brewery. Here the girls had lunch including Danish frankfurters and potato salad, this rather odd meal becoming a firm favourite of one of the girls. The Choir sang a few songs of appreciation between courses.

The next stop was the Commemorative park where two of the senior girls laid a wreath to members of the Danish underground who died during the war, then it was on to Hillerod for a visit to Frederiksborg Castle. 5pm was time for tea and a short concert at the International Folk High School at Elsinore. The Choir arrived back at Copenhagen at 8pm and some of the girls still had the energy to go dancing and dining until lam at the National Scala.

Friday morning was rehearsal time at the Danish State Radio followed by lunch in the canteen. In the afternoon the girls visited the Zoological Gardens, had tea and sang. They then had to make their own way back to their various hosts which was rather nerve wracking. Two girls had their addresss on a piece of paper which they showed to the tram driver in the hope that he would put them off at the right place; they did get back safely.

The two Choirs met at 7pm for another rehearsal at Broadcasting House and then sang in the concert hall from 8pm until 9.30pm. An enthusiastic audience heard a mixture of grand opera, English ballads and a Danish song "Barcarolle" which the Choir had learnt especially for the tour and Jill Taylor introduced the items in Danish. There were two groups of songs by the Studenter Sangforeningen, beautiful renderings of Danish and English part songs.

When the actual broadcasting had finished the Scottish dancers of the Choir danced the Highland Fling while the rest sang "The Keel Row". The two Choirs then joined in singing both the British and Danish national anthems.

At the end of the concert, much to the amusement of the Choir, a huge wreath of oak leaves was placed on Mr Davies's shoulders. A European custom signifying that a great honour is bestowed. On the tour Mr Davies also had to get used to being presented with a bouquet of flowers at the end of each performance.

After the concert there was supper and a party at the Restaurant Karnappen attended by the student hosts and their ladies, as well as the English party. The Mayor Ald. H.C.Janes presented the students with a Union Jack on a marble base, suitably inscribed "From the Mayor and Corporation of Luton". Mr Davies was made an honorary member of the Studenter Sangforeningen and given a membership badge.

On Saturday the girls left at 9.30am for Soro, stopping en route to see the cathedral at Roskilde. There was a delay to enable the girls to see the Danish King and Queen who were also visiting the cathedral, so this meant an alteration to the schedule. It was a rather hurried journey to the lakeside Restaurant Parnas for an excellent English lunch with the Mayor of Soro and Mr Otto Leinsner, a famous Danish radio star.

It was then on by boat to Soro to be greeted by the Scandinavian Airlines Band. Lining up in fours the girls walked proudly in procession behind the Band through streets lined with people waving both the Danish flag and the Union Jack. The Luton girls made a colourful picture in their smart blue dresses and blazers as they followed the Band in uniforms of navy and silver. There was an official welcome, the Band played God Save the Queen and in return the Choir sang the Danish National Anthem. This was followed by a concert in the Frater Garten of the Soro Akademi and tea in the Domestic Science School hall. Here the Headmistress congratulated the girls on their singing but said they must also leam how to cook and look after their future husbands.

That evening back in Copenhagen, the girls amused themselves, some going dancing at the "Pearl of the Coast" about 30 miles outside Copenhagen

The English Church of St. Albans in Groningen was their first stop on Sunday morning where the choir sang "Panis Angelicus" before returning to have lunch with their host families. Jill Taylor was also asked to record an interview with one of the students for a broadcast.

At their afternoon concert in the Tivoli Gardens, the Choir had to get used to the slow hand clap being a sign of appreciation, not disapproval as in England. Dinner was at the Wivex Restaurant, one of the best in Copenhagen, as guests of the gramophone companies Skandinavisk Grammophon A/S and Skandinavisk Odeon A/S where representatives of HMV and Parlophone made speeches of welcome. It was while the girls were enjoying this meal that the famous Tivoli Guard paraded in their honour. Following a short concert Jill Taylor was presented with a bouquet of carnations by the Studenter as a "Thank you" for her job as announcer and a firework show organised by the management brought the evening to a close.

Monday was time to move on. In the morning the girls went shopping and then attended a farewell lunch. There were the usual speeches and Mr Davies presented a silk pocket handkerchief to each of the Studenter and an ashtray was given to their president Mr K.O. Buch. By 2.20pm the choir were on their way to Odense, the birthplace of Hans Christian Andersen.

They arrived at 7 pm. to be met by a large crowd. So many people wanted to entertain the English visitors that the girls were to be billeted singly in over 70 homes, quite an ordeal for most of the girls as this was their first trip to a foreign country. Yvonne James felt rather lonely as her hosts could not speak English. However, the next morning she cheered up immensely when her place at breakfast was surrounded by birthday presents. She did find it strange to have a mug of hot chocolate for breakfast. "Not her cup of tea" she said.

Josie Fisher was lucky as her hosts, the Willert family, all spoke English and her niece Marie stayed with Svend Larson, curator of the Hans Christian Andersen

Museum. Margaret Oakley stayed with the Rasmussen family and later corresponded with their son Lars for over a year. Rita Sygrove possibly had the most unusual digs, as she was presented with a bicycle to ride to her billet. With her luggage strapped on the back, she followed her host on the fourteen miles home; it took them 1 1/2 hours. She described it as a "Hill Billy farm" and when the farmer belched after his food to show his appreciation, he was disappointed that Rita did not follow suit, thinking she had not enjoyed her meal. Rita forgot her TV dress for one performance and Mr Davies told her to cycle back to the farm to collect it and then cycle back for the concert. She said "No" very firmly and from then on she had a taxi.

One girl remembers having pigeon for her meal and while she was eating she was thinking of those in Trafalgar Square and was not sure she really fancied it. Another girl was out dancing again with her hosts until 11pm.

There was a 9am start to a busy Tuesday. In the morning a wreath laying ceremony, at the graves of British and Canadian airmen killed during the war, was followed by a short rehearsal at 9.30 am. and then a tour of the new town hall. In the afternoon there was a visit to the Hans Christian Andersen museum followed by a very successful evening concert. In spite of the choir singing two extra songs the audience were reluctant to go and applauded for a long time.

Pretty girls were bound to attract the attention of the Danish young men and while the girls were in Odense they heard that two members of the Choir had "captured the hearts" of two lads from Copenhagen. These two boys had cycled, then hitch hiked from Copenhagen to Odense without a kroner in their pockets to meet "two of the sweetest girls they had ever met". Anxious parents reported the boys as missing and the police caught up with them in Odense.

The girls were worried about the incident appearing in the papers but Mr Davies said it was good publicity for the Choir. Later, one of the girl's mothers was rather surprised to read about her daughter's follower in the Luton News.

The two boys were not the only people to be impressed with the girls. One of the local papers, "Fyns Socialdemokrat" carried the following:- "The Luton Girls Choir. They are very clever and charming those 72 English girls who are touring Denmark. The one who heard them sing over the wireless had clear understanding that the Luton Girls Choir is a most well instructed and well trained choir, but only personal acquaintance in the concert hall confirmed convincingly the quality of the Choir".

Another early start on Wednesday as the Choir enjoyed further sightseeing before leaving at 1 pm for Aarhus, the last stage of their tour. More new families as the girls were met at the station by their hosts.

Thursday it was another town and another town hall. The locals in Aarhus referred to their town hall as "Sing Sing" because of its forbidding appearance and revoloutionary design; however the Choir were given an excellent reception and they sang for the dignitaries in the council chamber.

The girls then assembled at the local churchyard while Mr and Mrs Davies laid a wreath to the men of the R.A.F. who had lost their lives locally during the war. Lunch and dinner were with the host families, with a visit to the old town at Vesterbrogade in the afternoon.

The final concert was in the town's magnificent university where the overwhelming demand for tickets could not be satisfied. The building was full and people even crowded on the window balconies and on the steps of the hall to listen. During the evening the Choir presented Mr and Mrs Davies with a travelling clock as a 29th wedding anniversary present.

There was also the presentation of a solid silver antique powder compact to Agnete Binfield, a charming 20 year old Danish girl. Jean Fountain and Peggy Coggins were billeted with her parents in Copenhagen and as Agnete was studying languages she had been very helpful to the Choir. She became very popular and was asked to accompany them for the rest of their tour.

Friday was their last day and in the morning there was a coach tour of Aarhus, then in the afternoon the girls went shopping for souvenirs. Later that evening, Alderman and Mrs Janes gave a dinner party for the adult members of the tour to celebrate their wedding anniversary. They received some hand embroidered handkerchiefs as a present from the Choir.

On Saturday the Choir began their homeward journey on the train from Aarhus. Over 200 people came to see them off and the station master shook hands with each of the girls. Just as the train was leaving he called over the loud speaker "Good luck Luton girls and may you have a safe journey home".

The Sunday crossing was reasonably smooth; the Mayor held a service in the morning, in the afternoon the Choir sang to the other passengers. During the tour the hosts had been so welcoming and the girls were loaded with presents ranging from a beautiful necklace to a side of bacon. Mr Davies advised the girls to be honest and to declare everything but there was no bother from the Customs men. They just wanted the Choir to sing, so the girls obliged with "Count your Blessings".

The girls had done a lot of impromptu singing as they travelled around and the Danish press described them as "the finest ambassadors sent to this country in 23 years". As a memento of their trip the Mayor presented all the girls with a small Royal Copenhagen porcelain dish, decorated with a picture of Copenhagen Town Hall.

Parents and Supporters Association.

The idea of a Parents Association to support Choir activities had been tossed around for some time before 1953 but it came to fruition when the Choir was able to arrange the visit to Denmark. While it was under discussion various parents had agreed to take positions of responsibility but their girls left the Choir and so the parents' interest waned.

The objectives of the Association were :- to give support and assistance to the Choir and to enable the parents of Choir members to meet socially and so get to know each other better. Financial assistance was given with the intention of relieving some of the burden imposed on Mr Davies.

The parents were canvassed to join and nearly all did so. There was a committee meeting about once a fortnight and Bring and Buy and Jumble Sales were held at intervals. Gradually both financial and practical help were given to the Choir. When the Whitley Bay Choir came to Luton in 1956 the Parents Association was asked to help find accommodation for the girls and when the Choir went to Australia the Association had enough money to hire a coach for the parents to go to Heathrow to bid farewell to their girls. The parents remained active as a group while the girls were away and shared information and letters from the travellers. The Association was still raising money while the girls were in Australia and on their return there was enough in the funds to provide a welcome home Christmas buffet and Dance at the George Hotel.

At first the Association used Christchurch Hall for its sales but later the venue changed to Bury Park Memorial Hall. The offficers also changed over the years but the function remained the same. In 1968 the secretary made an impassioned speech at one of the Bazaars, complaining that the town did not support the Choir and did not even attend the concerts in large numbers. He said the vast majority of people were not Lutonians and had never heard of the Choir; the controversy even made the national press.

The Association provided food and refreshments at the annual Watford concert and in the programme for the 16th November 1969, a Gala Rhapsody, a note said the Association had contributed £450 towards the £800 needed for new dresses, as well as making donations to the Choir's Trust during the previous years. Members prepared the food and drink for 200 performers and at an average concert would wash up 1000 cups and at least 500 plates.

The Parents Association went by coach to most of the venues close to Luton, paying their own way. Occasionally they would go by coach on one of the weekend tours or it might be that just a few parents would travel by car and put up in hotels at the resort.

The last chairman of the Association was George Goodman, whose two girls were both members of the Choir. He felt that both his girls and he and his wife got a lot of pleasure from the Choir's activities. He in turn was able to be of help to Mr Davies who was finding the going rather tough towards the end.

The rest of 1953 followed the general pattern of concerts away at the weekend and more local performances on week day evenings. In Northampton when they sang at the Central Methodist Church, the girls found the October "Church Bulletin" was devoted solely to a feature on the Choir. The Mayor and Mayoress, Alderman and Mrs H.C. Janes invited the Choir to an "at home" at the Town Hall on November 30th and in December they appeared at Watford in a Henry Hall's Guest night. In true Henry Hall fashion there was no indication of performers until the evening, as the surprise was supposed to be part of the enjoyment.

That Christmas Mr and Mrs Davies's card featured a scene from the pageant and the words "Christmas in Merrie England".

The following year, Whitsun 1954, found the Choir on their furthest trip north when their tour took them as far as Scotland. Again it was a very hectic weekend, all concerts being sponsored by the National Children's Home. The music was rather more classical than usual, although the programmes did include "Charlie is my Darling" and the highland dancing group also performed. The girls left Luton on Saturday 5th of June going first to London and then by train and coach to Middlesborough. There they sang in the Town Hall and after staying the night as usual in private homes the girls travelled on to Durham. Sunday was a busy day with an afternoon recital and an evening concert at Bond Gate Church in Darlington. On Monday the Choir travelled still further north to Paisley. There the concert was in the Central Hall and the guest of honour was Sir George Laidlaw, a member of the Board of Governors of the BBC Scottish Region. Some of the girls spent the night in Paisley while others journeyed on to Glasgow, one of the treats on the way being a meal near Ben Nevis. On Tuesday the Choir was reunited for a tour of the lochs and although the weather was not very favourable they were able to have lunch on the romantic banks of Loch Lomond.

The Choir's final performance was in Glasgow. First they had a special reception from the Lord Provost and his wife and then there was a tea when the Choir were joint guests of honour with the evangelist Billy Graham. Many of the girls have souvenir pictures of the great man in his plastic mac as he posed in the rain. Music Librarian, Anne Norcross, can remember having to go by taxi, with the transport manager Mr Bush, to get some music specially requested by Billy Graham.

The highlight of their tour was a performance in the world famous St Andrews Hall on the Tuesday night. Afterwards there was no time to recover as it was all aboard the night train to Euston station. Coaches met them in London and took them on to Luton where all the girls were either back home or at work by 9.30am Wednesday morning. Not a restful weekend but another collection of happy memories. One girl had a novel experience when she stayed with her hosts in Glasgow. They were an elderly couple living in one of the tenement blocks and the Choir girl slept in a cupboard bed in the kitchen. She said it was quite a climb to get into but warm and cosy once she did so.

In July the Choir were on tour again, this time to Torquay where they gave nine performances in aid of St Luke's Church. The Church had been given 5 years in which to make itself self supporting and 1954 was the final year. In that time the congregation had risen from under a dozen to between six and seven hundred. The

Having tea with Billy Graham in Glasgow. Photo Planet News.

concerts were held in the town hall and as it was renowned for its poor acoustics Mr Davies had visited it the previous May to see what improvements could be made. He arranged for a temporary stage to be erected, with a canopy in front, and the reception was much better.

There were four different programmes spread over the nine performances and the programmes for the concerts were in various colours, with the individual details on separate insets. Small potted biographies of each singer were given and the pianist, Sir Francis Cassel, was the guest artiste.

The Choir were very well received in the area. When the managing director and the editor in chief of the Torbay Herald Express read their critic's report of the singing, they were so impressed that they travelled from Plymouth to hear for themselves.

During the week of concerts there were many opportunities for gifts of appreciation. Mr Davies received a desk calendar and a silver inkpot from the sponsors, Mrs Davies was given a bouquet of flowers by St Luke's Girls Choir, Sir Francis was given a desk barometer and each of the girls had a box of chocolates. Many letters of thanks and congratulations were received after the tour.

St Luke's magazine, like others before, featured the Choir's visit in some detail. Names and addresses of the hosts, with the names of their guest were given, together with a list of people who had made a generous donation; even the amount was shown. As the girls stayed with their hosts for a week there were various amusing incidents recalled. Two members stayed in a residential home for elderly ladies; their bedroom was in the attic and their "en suite" was a sink. While washing their precious nylons, they lost them down the plug hole, there being no waste trap. After a mad charge down three flights of stairs into the garden they were able to rescue the stockings unscathed from the garden drain.

That particular tour seemed to be dogged by unpleasant happenings. On the journey to Devon the Choir had been held up by an accident and a fire. During their stay, one girl caught Scarlet Fever and had to be moved to the isolation hospital while another member caught Chicken Pox and had to stay longer, the others sharing her digs were checked each day in case they too succumbed. Mrs Bush, who was travelling with the Parents and Supporters, had to have an emergency operation for appendicitis and several of the girls got badly sunburnt.

Three of the Choir stayed in a large Edwardian House owned by two spinster sisters who were looked after by a housekeeper and a gardener. The sisters could not even boil an egg for themselves but the food was very plentiful, with raspberries and cream every day. When the Vicar came for tea it was a typical Edwardian presentation with delicate cucumber sandwiches.The home had not been modernised and it was bed by candle light. Of course the girls were sure the house was haunted and every time anybody wanted to go to the bathroom they all lit their candles and went together. When the sisters attended the concert they arrived in a large hire car and waited for the girls after the show to take them home. The girls

Dancers at The Star and Garter Home, 1962. Photo from Library Collection.

described the week as living in a different era. Some years later one of the young guests met the housekeeper and her husband on a touring holiday near Lake Como. The housekeeper said the sisters had paid for her tour.

Two girls stayed longer in Torquay for a short holiday and were invited to sing at the church service the following Sunday. They obliged by singing "Ave Maria" as a duet. All the girls obviously enjoyed their week and were able to help St Lukes Church in its quest for self suffficiency.

As well as singing to raise money for charities, the Choir often sang to entertain groups of disadvantaged people. For several years they visited the British Legion Star and Garter Home in Richmond to sing for the disabled ex service people who were making the poppies for Remembrance Day. There would be a dinner first and then a social evening with the Choir and other entertainers providing the entertainment, the organisation responsible for hiring the performers being known as the Camel Corps. The evening was quite informal and there were lots of opportunities for community singing with items such as "I Belong to Glasgow", "Ship Ahoy", and "Goodbyee". The girls always enjoyed visiting the home and on their first visit in October 1954 they were also shown round the workshops. Their second concert was quite soon afterwards in March 1955.

In May there were concerts at Bournemouth and Weymouth and during the summer there were the usual seaside shows. They made their seventh appearance at Margate and on Sunday September 4th three coach loads of Choir and supporters arrived at Worthing at lunch time, performed to a near capacity audience in the Pier Pavilion in the evening and left again for Luton immediately after the show. Programmes were now featuring the grouping as used on the television and Mr Davies was also playing Chaminade's "Automne", a special arrangement by Glaister Newton for the Choir.

On September l9th, the 15th anniversary of the Battle of Britain, the Choir sang in a TV programme called "Garrison Theatre" from Biggin Hill in Kent. Vera Lynn, Bob Monkhouse and the Squadronaires also appeared in the programme which began a week of celebrations.

A novel form of publicity occurred for the "Scarlet and Blue" concert in Northampton on October 9th. Each evening for four days before the concert two Irish Guardsmen in full ceremonial dress stood sentry in the foyer of the theatre. They were there both to promote Army recruiting and to publicise the "Scarlet and Blue" concert.

The visit to Oswestry in Shropshire on October 22nd and 23rd had strange origins. Two brothers had been billeted with Mr Davies' mother during the First World War. One brother had been killed but the other had kept in touch with the Davies family over the years and when an Oswestry group were raising funds to provide a playground in memory of a local girl, Patricia Needham, the brother's daughter contacted Mr Davies to see if the Choir could help. They sang at two concerts, one on Saturday and one on Sunday and also had tea with the girl's parents on Saturday afternoon.

January 1956 saw another TV appearance, this time on the BBC programme "Forces Request" hosted by Josephine Douglas. She was interviewing servicemen overseas and when one of the soldiers asked for the "Happy Wanderer" it was sung by the Choir in the studio in England. There were many close ups while the song was being sung and lots of delighted Luton residents as they recognised a friend or member of the family.

Wilfred Pickles did not endear himself to the Choir in March 1956. The Choir and the Irish guards were at the Royal Albert Hall in a "Blue Rhapsody" concert, the compere being Wilfred Pickles assisted by Mrs Pickles and dog. He refused to attend the rehearsal so Jill Taylor had to act as stand in, and when 12 of the Choir left the stage to later appear in costume for "Choir of Angels" he said they were just going to put on their night wear. Coupled with his remark of "Did you pay the audience to come?" Mr Pickles was not the Choir's most favourite person.

The North of England also had a girls choir in the '50s, from Whitley Bay in Northumberland. In April 1956 on Saturday 14th, together with the Central Band of the R.A.F., the two Choirs joined forces at a concert in Luton called "On Wings of Song". The girls from Whitley Bay wore white evening dresses with red boleros, sashes and gloves, the Luton girls were in their ice blue. The conductor of the Northern Choir was Bill Armstrong and the Band was conducted by Wing Commdr. A.E. Sims. There was a total of 150 girls as the Choirs sang, both separately and together.

In the programme was a photograph of 17 Luton girls with the longest service and the names of two others who could not attend the sitting; other Choir members were listed in order of joining. There were photos of the Whitley Bay Choir and the three conductors.

The concert was held in the Methodist Church in Chapel Street and a programme note said that cars could park in Regent Street and New Street without lights, by kind permission of the Luton Superintendent of Police.

On Sunday there was a similar concert at Watford Town Hall. Jill Taylor was the Luton commere and Shirley Heppie introduced her Choir in the Whitley Bay items. At Watford the Stone's Fashion Cup for the most popular and hardworking girl was awarded that year to Anne Norcross.

Whitsun weekend was spent in Bournemouth at the Winter Gardens, another "On Wings of Song" with Wing Commdr. A.E. Sims and the Central Band of the Royal Airforce. Quite a costume affair, twelve members of the Choir dressed as angels for the "Evening Prayer" from Hansel and Gretel; the soloists Gillian Wicks and Hazel Newton and the four girls in the Highland dancing display were also in

The Stones Cup, presented annually to the most outstanding girl in the Choir. Photo Bob Norman.

costume. On the Saturday night it was the wardrobe mistress, Mary Davie's final concert and she presented Mr and Mrs Davies with a musical Toby Jug which played the Blue Danube. On Sunday Beryl Brown's solo, the "Jewel Song" from Faust, received so much applause, the audience would not stop until she sang again, thus breaking one of Mr Davies's rules about soloists and encores.

In July the Choir appeared on TV with George Melachrino, singing for part of the time in "Summer Serenade" and their TV appearance in "Arenascope" in August had very mixed reviews. The show was a "ladies only" with a cast of over a hundred, such items as Sheila Van Damm and Carole Carr competing against Pat Moss and Sylvia Peters, in car control and wheel changing. The WRAF physical training team gave a display and as well as the Choir other musical contributors were the Dagenham Girl Pipers and Gracie Cole and her all women orchestra. Although supposedly an all women show, Kenneth Horne and Richard Murdoch were brought in to judge the beauty competition and Mr Davies of course was conducting the Choir. The girls wore various coloured kimonos and flowers in their hair while they sang the "Humming Chorus" from Madame Butterfly, with Joan Hammond. Nobody seemed to like the programme; some critics said the Choir were good, others said they were lost in the overall show.

Finances were a little strained in 1957 and the Choir gave a "Blue Rhapsody" concert in Luton Community Centre instead of in London. There was no band, just the Choir and the Choral Society with Guest Artiste Harold Smart at the Hammond organ. Mr Davies was anxious to have as many girls singing as possible because there were lots of mums and dads in the audience to hear them, a rare Luton appearance so more families could come to listen. It was at this concert that Mr Davies announced that six records would be produced under the "Blue Rhapsody" label with the proceeds going to the National Children's Home.

April 19th - 22nd was an Easter tour of the West Country. The Choir, parents and friends travelled to Cornwall on Friday, stopping at Stonehenge en route for a picnic. Their first concert was in the evening at Taunton Methodist Church. An audience of 1100 had to be restrained in their applause because it was Good Friday. At Helston on Saturday the delighted audience was not restrained when it joined the Choir in singing its local song, "The Floral Dance". There were two concerts on Sunday; in the afternoon they sang at St Ives Methodist Church and in the evening they appeared at Holman's Canteen in Camborne. Again the local people joined in as the Choir sang the rather strange Camborne Town song :- "Going up Camborne Hill - coming down, The horses stood while the wheels went round, Going up Camborne Hill - coming down". There were roars of approval from the audience. The concert on Easter Monday in Falmouth was also very popular and had been sold out days in advance. The programmes listed all the names of the girls who were touring and with five concerts in four days it was a heavy tour for a holiday week end. The cost was over £700 and the girls stayed in the Sun Court Hotel Falmouth. On the last night the proprietor made them traditional Cornish pasties as a special treat. One of the Luton News reporters wrote that if Lutonians could see how the girls were received in other towns it might help them to appreciate the Choir more.

About this time, as they faced the challenge of skiffle groups, Mr Davies was quoted as saying the Choir does not want to sing "Rock and Roll" on stage. They will continue to make records for people who are lovers of well written music and well known classics. He bemoaned the fact that tickets for a choral concert cost 2/6 and 5/- while for skiffle they were 25/- and there was a queue a mile long to get in.

The annual concert at Worthing saw the retirement of one of the longest serving members of the Choir. Patricia Corley had joined at nine years old and sung for fourteen and a half years in the Choir. As the minimum age for joining was later raised, nobody else would equal this amazing record. She sang the solo "Abide with Me" especially for Mr Davies and as she received her clock she presented him with a musical toilet roll holder.

The programme now featured a section called "pop ballads" and included such items as "A House with Love in it", "Kindness" and various songs from the USA. During the concert Mr Davies asked overseas visitors to join him on stage and there were people from Germany, India, Australia, South America and South Africa. He promised to send them all a copy of the Choir's latest record. Marion Large, who had married the Irish Guardsman Bob Oades, accompanied the Choir to Worthing and joined them in singing a selection from "Glamorous Night".

At the end of the year there was a flu epidemic and the Choir were stretched to meet their commitments. They sang at Houghton Regis with only 41 singers and at Coventry with 62. This did give some of the younger new members a chance to sing as soloists and Mr Davies rearranged the groupings. He said he had never let anybody down yet and he did not intend to. The programmes were advertising the Choir's records, suggesting they would make nice Christmas presents and there was a detachable order slip which could be used at a local record shop.

The "Blue Rhapsody" concert at Watford in February 1958 was a delayed "coming of age" celebration for the Choir. The Irish Guards had been on a world tour in 1957 so the Choir waited for their return. The Mayor and Mayoress Alderman and Mrs S C Haynes and 500 Lutonians, friends and relatives of the two Choirs, filled 11 coaches and joined the celebrations at the Watford Town Hall. The Luton Girls Choir now featured a spot for the "Lutones", three of the senior sopranos, who sang "Tammy" one of the top songs of the day. They were rather envied by the other girls. The Olivestone cup went to Barbara Chance that year. She only missed 1 of 400 concerts and 2 of 1,000 rehearsals.

At Bournemouth, Whitsun 1958 the Choir appeared with the Band of the Royal Artillery for the first time. Seventy two girls spent the weekend there with a concert on the Saturday and the Sunday. The biggest hit on the programme was the new burlesque item "The Musicians" where several girls dressed up and took off various musical instruments.

In September there was a special concert at the Victoria Palace Theatre organised by the Grand Order of Water Rats. It was a tribute to Arthur Whelan who at 80 years old had just had a leg amputated. A star studded cast included Max Bygraves, the Beverley Sisters, Anne Shelton, Charlie Chester and Tommy Trinder as well as the Luton girls. They were most excited by the new star Frankie Vaughan and gave him a rapturous welcome. The Choir sang two numbers from the time Arthur Whelan was at the peak of his career, "My Heart and I" and a selection from "Tales from the Vienna Woods". Their third item was "Wouldn't it be Luverly".

The girls were most disappointed that they could not attend the party afterwards as they were not professional show people.

In June 1958 the possibility of an Australasian Tour was discussed and later the songs included in various concerts were being learnt for the tour. The commeres were also the girls who later were to do the job in Australia.

There were TV appearances in May when the Choir was one of the guests on the Jewel and Warris Show and in November when they were in "Chelsea at 9". In the Musical Memories section the guest was the composer Hans May who recalled some of the songs which made him famous. The Choir sang Queen Mary's favourite, "Break of Day" and off screen they backed Joan Hammond in the entrance of "Madame Butterfly".

At the beginning of 1959 there was intense preparation for the forthcoming tour. The date was put back to August to coincide with the Royal visit of Princess Alexandra for the Queensland Centenary Celebrations and New Zealand was included in the itinerary. Some concerts were given in the proceeding months and Mr Davies rose from his sick bed, after an attack of flu, to take the Choir to Scunthorpe in February. There were concerts for the National Children's Home in Dover and Ashford, and also their annual visit to sing for the patients at the Star and Garter Home. On June 6th 1959 the Choir made one of their, by now, rare appearances on television. To celebrate 5 years of Eurovision, twelve countries combined in a 75 minute programme, "Vision On Europe". Four grand pianos played the "Warsaw Concerto", David Hughes sang a solo specially written for him while the Choir acted as backing. There was a whole day's rehearsal in London and the show went out live in the evening.

Chapter Ten

Hospital Singing

The Choir always spent the morning of the 25th December singing in the local hospital. At first it was at the old Bute Hospital near Dallow Road. The girls would sing in the long corridor with the wards leading off on each side; there would be both carols and Christmas songs.

Later they moved to the Luton and Dunstable Hospital which was on the outskirts of town and initially there was no transport available, so the girls were expected to get there as best they could. Betty Bird and her friend Grace walked from Park Square and Connie Chandler can remember walking from Kingsway in the snow. It just did not occur to any of the girls not to go. Later buses were provided by volunteer crews from Luton Corporation to transport the girls.

The Choir sang for 8 to 10 minutes in every ward, a piano being pushed round to accompany them. By the time they had finished, the turkeys were being carved by a doctor for dinner. Each Christmas, George Gurney of the Luton News would take a photograph of the girls singing at the hospital.

During one visit a member of the Choir actually had to use the service instead of providing the entertainment. She had previously injured her wrist in a car accident and thought it was just badly sprained. A nurse spotted that it was looking rather nasty and before she knew what was happening the girl was having her arm set and plastered. She was then taken home by Mr Davies to sleep off the anaesthetic.

Anne Norcross can remember one lady asking the Choir to sing "The Holy City". The Choir were happy to oblige but by the time they had finished the lady had peacefully passed away. Anne did not feel like eating her Christmas lunch that year.

December was also the time for an annual visit to Buckinghamshire, always to Stoke Mandeville in the evening, with a concert at one of the other hospitals in the area during the afternoon.

For several years the Choir sang at Stone Hospital for mentally handicapped people. The Choir would contribute sweets and one of the coach drivers, Ted, would dress up as Father Christmas and distribute small parcels to the patients. Julie Barrett looks back on these visits as time well spent and feels the people really responded to the Choir. Most of the girls felt moved at this time and many mentioned these visits in their memories.

In December 1955 the Choir were singing to injured soldiers at the Military Hospital in Wheatley, some of whom had just returned from Cyprus, Malaya and Kenya. The girls were booked to sing outside two wards but were asked to extend the visit and also sing outside the ward for serious cases. One soldier was so ill he could only breathe with the help of oxygen and he asked if the Choir would sing a song especially for him. It was thought he only had a few days to live but luckily he was able to have an operation and he pulled through. He later wrote to Mr Davies and then corresponded with one of the girls for some time. The girls later had tea at the hospital, enjoying a special Christmas cake decorated in the Choir colours.

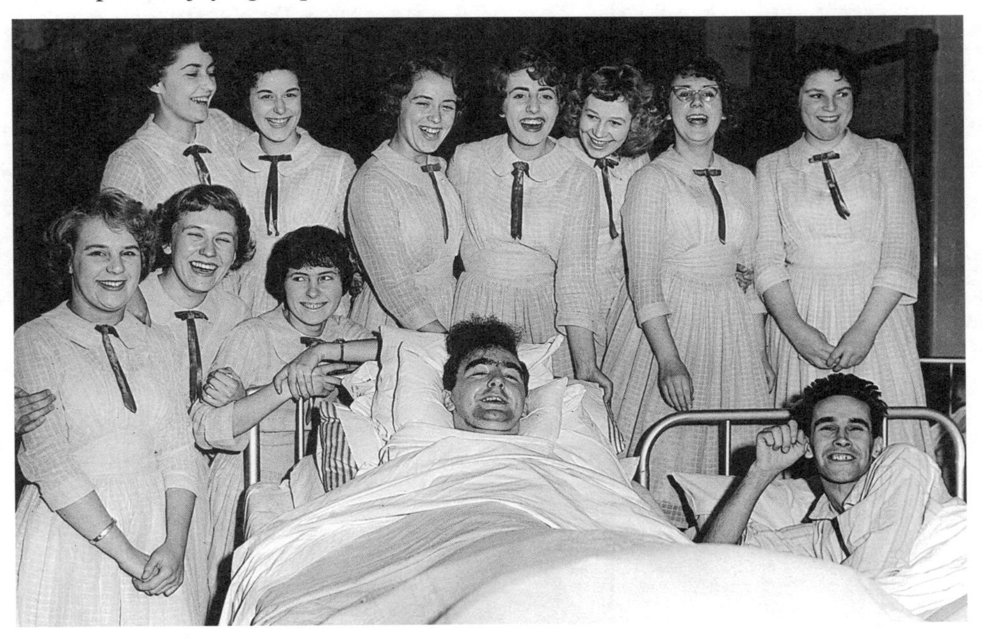

Singing at Stoke Mandeville Hospital. Photo Department of Clinical Photography, Stoke Mandeville Hospital.

The evening concert was in Stoke Mandeville as usual where they sang in the gymnasium to an audience of 500. The concert was also relayed to the other patients throughout the rest of the hospital. The girls then sat down to a three course meal. It was at Stoke Mandeville where the Choir met one of their biggest fans. Mr Davies said he had a surprise for them and into the rehearsal walked Jimmy Saville. They were singing at the hospital on one of the evenings that he was working as a volunteer porter and this is his description, written in 1999, of the meeting that neither he nor the girls will forget.

"A million years ago, when I worked down the coal mines in Yorkshire, I heard a recording of the Luton Girls Choir singing "Stranger in Paradise". What the magic of the music was, I don't know. It was music to close your eyes and get lost in. A rare feeling for a teenage coal miner. All through the Top of the Pops and Radio One Days, when asked my favourite group, it was the same answer, The Luton Girls Choir. Newspapers and magazines laughed, but I had the last laugh because I actually was telling the truth, for once! Imagine my shock when, twenty years later, walking into Stoke Mandeville Hospital and finding the LGC was giving a concert for the patients and staff. It blew my mind. I rushed into the rehearsal and there was much screaming and carry on as TV's Mr Top of the Pops appeared. They flatly refused to believe I was their No. 1 fan. What a great afternoon and evening. What a laugh. I taught them a naughty ditty and they sang it with great gusto as I waved their coach off. A lifetime memory to this day".

Jimmy Saville had a programme called "Saville's Travels" on BBC 1 at the time and recorded interviews with the girls at Stoke Mandeville subsequently featured in the show.

In later years the Choir also sang at hospitals in Harpenden but they continued to sing each Christmas Day at the Luton and Dunstable Hospital, their final visit being in 1975, their last public performance with Mr Davies.

Chapter Eleven

Tour of Australasia

The highlight of the Choir's 40 years must be the trip to Australia and New Zealand in 1959. An enormous undertaking in the days when foreign travel was not as common as it is now. A trip in 1950 had been turned down because the terms were not acceptable and there had been little time for organisation. That year the Australian Broadcasting system had produced a simulated radio tour featuring the Luton Girls Choir. A Miss Peggy Hamilton Broad of the Australian Broadcasting Company visited England, watched the Choir rehearsing and made notes re the Choir's activities. The whole programme was to imitate as faithfully as possible the activities of the Choir giving a concert, from the time they left their homes until they returned to Luton after the show. An actress in the Australian studio imitated the girls arriving to board the coach for the tour. Somebody else was the "voice" of Mr Davies, reading exact words spoken by him. Listeners were told of the Choir's visit to the Mansion House and St Paul's Cathedral and they heard two items from that concert. An article on the Choir, by Miss Broad, also appeared in the Australian equivalent of the Radio Times.

In 1952 a promotional tape had been sent to New Zealand and was broadcast on New Zealand radio, hoping this might bring offers of a trip. It was however a call in 1957 from Lew Levisohn, Winifred Attwell's husband, that finally put the wheels in motion.

A company "Lew Levisohn Presentations" was formed and then sub let to other entrepreneurs. The Queensland government were involved, because of their centenary celebrations, with Laurie E. Smith Pty. Ltd. looking after that area. David N. Martin Pty. Ltd. in association with Edgley and Dawe and John Neary Pty. Ltd. were the entrepreneurs for Sydney, Adelaide, Melbourne and Perth. R.J.Kerridge of Kerridge Odeon covered New Zealand. The agent was Jack Neary and the tour manager for both Australia and New Zealand was Lloyd Ravenscroft. The trip was originally planned for April and May but was later changed to August and the three month trip was estimated to cost £80,000. Although it was a commercial enterprise there was a lot of local planning to do. Negotiations included a luncheon conference for all the employers of the girls, as their co-operation was needed in granting three months leave of absence. This was readily agreed in all but one case, The Abbey National Building Society. The girl in question resigned her job so that she could go on the trip. Forty seven girls were to travel, plus Mr and Mrs Davies and Peggy Coggins. The cost was £1,420 per person so only the best could be chosen, who would that be? There were intensive rehearsals and after six months, auditions were held to select those fortunate enough to go.

The preliminary choice of 51 girls was based on their length of service with the Choir, followed by their ability, personality and general behaviour. The difficult choice of their singing fell to Mr Glaister Newton, a professional adjudicator engaged by Mr Davies. Test pieces were sung behind a screen so that looks would not influence the choice. He then chose 40 girls immediately but had to arrange a second audition to choose the other seven; several days of waiting and tension. There were 24 sopranos, 14 mezzo sopranos and 9 contraltos; 9 of the group were also soloists. All the girls were naturally delighted, some rearranging their life to go. Beryl Brown postponed her wedding and Linda Bunker, who was due to go to St Martins School of Art in the September, was able to delay entrance until the November. Jill Banks was glad the date had been changed as she had to have her tonsils removed. Barbara Chance just managed to go on the tour before she reached 24years old and had to retire. June Ekins wanted an Australian boyfriend and to fulfil her lifetime ambition of living on an Australian horse farm. She worked for Vauxhall Motors and had been sending messages to the company in Melbourne.

There followed many meetings of the Choir trustees, personal interviews and meetings with parents and numerous practical matters had to be dealt with. Insurance against illness or accident and the emergency return to England, in the event of a parent becoming ill, had to be considered. Also the possibility of a girl having to remain behind in any city owing to illness and eventually flying on to rejoin the party. There was no free health care in Australia or New Zealand, so heavy expenses could soon be incurred. As it was, only one girl was detained in hospital and the rest of the minor ailments such as colds, sore throats, ear infections, teeth extraction etc. totalled about £100. A visit to the doctor cost about 25/- (£1.25) or for a consultant or specialist 3 guineas (£3.30). In each town or city there was actually a doctor on call for the Choir if necessary.

Vaccinations against smallpox and cholera were also needed. These had a bad effect on Peggy Coggins, confining her to bed and causing her some trouble while she was actually in Australasia. She still managed to type letters of appeal to local businesses which resulted in enough money to buy each of the girls a Revelation Fibre Glass suitcase.

Accommodation, as on English tours, would be in private homes of people associated with musical organisations, schools, churches, Rotary clubs, The Victoria League, and The Association of Country Women of the World. Industrial contacts such as General Motors and Electrolux were also used.

A duplicate copy of the piano music of all the items in the repertoire was made by Vic Cherry, a draughtsman at Vauxhall. So many of the numbers which were specially written for the choir, including many by Glaister Newton, were not in published form so could not be easily replaced. One of the items from "Madame Butterfly" was to be sung in costume and during the tour specific girls were in charge of these and other stage costumes, making sure that they were packed safely in the correct boxes after each performance.

Several weeks before departure, rehearsals were being held almost every other night to ensure the Choir were on top form musically. "Waltzing Matilda", which was originally in the Choir repertoire, had lapsed, so had to be learnt by the new members. "Now is the Hour", based on a Maori song, was specially arranged for them.

Each girl had two pieces of luggage plus an overnight bag. These included the stone coloured Revelation fibreglass cases, lined with blue silk, bought from the money raised locally, each one having the girl's choir number on top in blue. The stage frocks were packed into five special trunks. In off duty hours the girls wore their own clothes and a selection of the dresses to be used when the Choir were singing was sent ahead for publicity displays in shop windows.

Many gifts were received from traders including a vanity case for each girl containing solid cologne, hand cream and soap leaves. Sun hats were made and presented by City Millinery of King St. Luton and there were three first aid boxes, with a supply of stomach tablets from Boots the Chemist. W.H.Cox lent a cine camera and Pauline Millard had 40 reels of film with which to record the tour. The cine film has since been made into a video and many of the girls now have a copy of this priceless souvenir. The girls took ash trays, in the shape of plastic boaters, displaying the Choir badge, to leave as small gifts with their hosts.

They were given £2.50 a week pocket money (3 Australian pounds). Personal spending money was transferred en bloc to Australia and New Zealand and Peggy had to draw money from banks in each town where they stayed and have paying out sessions. Collecting the money was a formal occasion and in Brisbane her host advised her to wear a hat and gloves when going to see the Bank Manager.

Publicity photos were taken by a professional theatre photographer and the choir had travelled to the London studio on Armistice day the previous year. It was rumoured that several boys took out insurance at £1 a head in case their girls left them for a bronzed Australian. If he lost her the boy would get £250.

During the tour the girls were divided into five groups, each with its own leader, who had to ensure her members were present when the Choir was ready to move. This helped to spread the load of responsibility.

On June 26th there was a farewell concert in the new Luton College of Technology. The programme read "This is the final local appearance of the Luton Girls Choir prior to three months tour of the Commonwealth Countries of Australia and New Zealand". In the programme Mr Davies wrote a letter of thanks to the town, past members and all in attendance and there was a slip asking people to give donations to Choir funds.

The concert was attended by Dr Charles Hill who wished the Choir well on their tour. He bade them "Bring back news of the Commonwealth for here we know too little of the Commonwealth of which this country is the centre". He told them "Be yourselves on this tour and the bonds that bind the Commonwealth will be all the stronger". The Mayor, Mrs R.O. Andrews also paid a public tribute to the Choir and expressed the town's good wishes for a happy and successful tour.

Many of the audience were farmers and their wives, who, prior to the concert, were entertained at the George Hotel by the Directors of Dunn's Farm Seeds Ltd. Mr Davies was their S.E. Midlands Regional Supervisor and at the dinner described the function as an evening of celebration for the record tonnage of seed corn sales for the 1958/9 season for his company. Ever the business man, he was mixing the two events. Mr Alec Olivestone, one of the Trustees, gave a farewell dinner to the Choir in Stone's restaurant in Wellington Street. Sir John Burgoyne, before proposing the toast, said "the Choir were embarking on a wonderful adventure and would be ambassadors of the feminine graces of the English people. The most attractive thing in the world was a well behaved girl". Maureen Rennie proposed a toast of thanks to Sir John and to Mr and Mrs Olivestone.

The day of departure dawned and the Choir left Luton after a Civic send off and each girl received a sprig of white heather from Patricia Corley. She worked with Peggy as secretary and was staying at the office in Luton to manage the affairs of the Choir and Mr Davies.

On the morning of Monday 17th August two coaches filled with girls and luggage and decorated with banners listing the places which the Choir would visit, left Luton. Crowds gathered outside the Town Hall and lined George Street, shoppers waved and people cheered from their doorways. Lunch was at Slough in the Adelphi Cinema and then it was on to London Airport where a coach load of parents and friends were waiting to say some tearful goodbyes.

Chairman of the Parents and Supporters Association, Mr Joe Grove, wrote a poem of 14 verses in honour of the occasion. These are the first and last verses :

We have just been to London to see our girls go,
In two shades of blue they really made a show.
Hat, gloves, shoes and handbag in white,
To everyone they made a good sight.

Let us be thankful for those girls dressed in blue,
They give to the world a jolly good do.
Let the town be happy and mighty proud
For the girls dressed in blue, Arthur Davies' crowd.

While the Choir was on tour regular bulletins were sent to the Luton News by Peggy Coggins. These were displayed in Farmer's music shop so that people could follow the Choir's progress.

The flight was on a plane belonging to K.L.M., Royal Dutch Airlines, who did them proud, although the actual journey took much longer than it would today. The girls had eaten their first meal on the plane with relish, but gradually with time changes and lack of exercise, appetites diminished. Breakfast was at 2am in Beirut

The start of the Australasia Tour, 1959. Photo Luton News.

where there was a three hour stop and many of the local population came out to meet them. Then it was on to Karachi and a short stop in the K.L.M. rest house known as the Midway Hotel. A seven hour flight was followed by a night at Calcutta's largest and best hotel, the Grand. Some of the girls were upset when they saw the conditions of hundreds of people sleeping on the pavements. The younger girls were paired off with the older ones for moral support but the strange sights, sounds, humid atmosphere and unusual smells meant that none of them got much sleep. Their first experience of the "Mysterious East".

An all day flight was followed by a 36 hour stop in the luxury Manila Hotel on the sea front, again courtesy of K.L.M. At the airport Mr Davies was given a red rose and each of the girls received an orchid as a welcome gift from the Young People's International Reception Committee. At the hotel came a new taste experience for most of the Choir, when the girls, feeling like film stars, were given ice cold drinks of crushed pineapple.

K.L.M. arranged a sightseeing tour which included lunch at the Taal Vista lodge and a church with an organ made of 950 bamboos. They heard Schubert's "Ave Maria" played on this amazing instrument. The land was being ploughed and harrowed under water ready for the rice planting and this was another first for the girls. They also saw pineapples, bananas and coconuts growing in profusion. Back at the hotel they tried a traditional Chinese meal eaten with chopsticks. Some of the younger ones did not like the strangeness of this and made do with apple pie and ice cream. It was probably at this meal that Julie Barrett caught the bug which left her too ill to take much part in the first few days of the Choir's activities in Australia.

Although the goods in the shops were expensive, all the girls had to buy a souvenir. After lunch the following day it was all aboard the plane for Biak, a small airport of rest huts. The idea was to stop at Biak and arrive at Brisbane at a convenient time for the greatest number of people to be there to welcome them.

On the flight the girls received many gifts from the airline including a writing compendium, toilet bags, travelling slippers and perfume. These are still kept as treasured mementoes by many of the girls. Some of them were worried about the free packets of cigarettes, thinking they would have to pay duty on them.

In spite of the carefully timed arrival in Brisbane it clashed with that of Princess Alexandra, due by launch on the river. She drew most of the crowds; however there was a musical welcome from a highland pipe band and Mrs Davies was presented with a basket of flowers. The girls were staying with members of the Brisbane Eisteddfod Junior Choir and a warm welcome from their hosts did much to dispel any homesickness. Although the girls were very tired and just wanted to sleep they were taken off by their hosts to various entertainments. Peggy Coggins was given a quick tour of the town and then taken to an agricultural show. A minor hiccup occurred when two girls had to be re-billeted after a week as their host's daughter caught mumps.

The Choir had four free days before their first concert and this gave them chance to settle down and get over their tiredness from the journey. There were some rehearsals and the press were much amused when the girls sang "Happy Birthday" to Beryl Brown as it was her 21st birthday. There was also plenty of time for the hosts to show off their country. Visits included the Lone Pine Koala Bear Sanctuary with much cuddling of bears and a visit to Surfers Paradise on the Gold Coast, so called because of all the wealthy people living there in luxurious homes.

The Brisbane session, lasting ten days, was presented in conjunction with the Oral Deaf Association. The girls were very nervous at their first appearance in the Brisbane Concert Hall which was vast. There was a large audience and the women were dressed for the event in their jewellery and furs.

There were ten concerts at the Festival Hall including three matinees for school children. The Choir also gave a performance in the Red Cross hall of the Greenslopes Repatriation Hospital, where as well as the audience of 250 patients and relatives in the hall, there were a further 250 captive in their beds, listening on the hospital radio.

There were six concerts in the towns of Toowomba, Ipswich and Southport. During one performance an audience of 5,000 school children were delighted when Mr Davies asked for a volunteer to sing a verse from "Waltzing Matilda" and a pet kangaroo called Matilda hopped onto the stage. In Ipswich they were also entertained to dinner by the Blackstone Ipswich Cambrian Choir and each girl was given her own badge to mark the occasion, while at Southport, Vauxhall employees were guests of General Motors at lunch in Lennons Hotel.

The State Governor of Queensland Col. Sir Henry Abel Smith and his wife Lady May gave a reception for the Choir at Government House and General Motors of Brisbane provided a fleet of Vauxhall cars to take the girls back to their hosts. Later, at Parliament House, Mr H.B.Taylor, Chairman of the Committee in Parliament, and his wife hosted another reception. It was here that Peggy, in an elegant hat borrowed from her hostess for the occasion, attended instead of Mr Davies as he was feeling unwell.

Some of the girls were also fortunate enough to meet Princess Alexandra when she left the official party on a visit to St John's Cathedral to chat with them. When she got back into the car she used the wrong door and sat on Sir Abel Smith's hat.

The Choir had learnt the "Alexandra Waltz" in honour of Princess Alexandra and they recorded it in Brisbane with "Waltzing Matilda" on the reverse. As this was organised in a hurry, there was no orchestra to back the Choir, only Mr Davies playing the piano. Not all the choir's reviews were favourable. One critic, P.A.Watt, was annoyed that there was so much "light" music in the programme and claimed the "sing 'em muck" school of thought on Australian tours went out years ago. He did however think that in songs that gave the girls opportunity of showing real mettle, they were delightful. Another critic Dr W. Lovelock seemed to agree with him about the choice of programme, complaining that many of the songs were of the "sugary sentimental type". A review by Frederick Rogers in the "Sunday Mail" was somewhat scathing with the words "Mr Davies will be well advised in future concerts to carefully restrict the solo items as these we have heard during the Brisbane visit seem to underline the truism that good choral singing can be achieved with a group of poor or at least very mediocre individual voices". However the "ordinary" people were very appreciative and the last concert in Brisbane consisted of items from previous programmes requested by the audience.

It was in Brisbane that the most serious mishap occurred when Sheila Land slipped in the swimming pool and badly chipped a bone in her left elbow. The tour manager and Peggy took her to the rather basic hospital for treatment. She had to stay there overnight but was then allowed to travel on with the Choir to Sydney where, after an operation, she spent four more days in hospital.

The reception at Sydney airport was much larger than in Brisbane. As well as about 500 people there were 17 TV and newsreel cameras plus radio and press reporters. The Hurstville Royalettes and the Rockdale District Marching Girls formed a guard of honour while an army band from the 18th AA regiment performed in their honour. The band played "Waltzing Matilda" and the girls sang "The Happy Wanderer".

Mrs Davies had an emotional reunion with her brother from Melbourne who had come up to Sydney to meet her; she had not seen him for 40 years. An ex Choir girl, who had later emigrated to Australia, was waiting to introduce her two daughters to the girls. Later she was interviewed on the radio giving her account of the reunion with Mr and Mrs Davies and then wrote to the Luton News describing events.

The following day, the Choir were given a grand reception at the Town Hall by the Lord Mayor of Sydney, Alderman H.F.Jensen, and were shown the plans for the new opera house. They also had a day at the TV studios preparing for their first Australian TV programme. They had three slots in TCN's Anniversary Spectacular and sang seven songs including the "Alexandra Waltz". General Motors were again generous and Mr Davies had a car put at his disposal during his stay in Australia.

There was a good public relations officer covering the tour in both Brisbane and Sydney and the publicity was tremendous. One Australian newspaper "The Sun" did a big spread with the girls appearing in many of the advertisements as well. They were described as "50 Glorious Voices". The paper also gave the Sydney addresses of 10 of the girls, who were then besieged with telephone calls from admiring boys. The boys were told to come to the stage door where they could be given the "once over". A Sydney paper did a six page supplement, broadcasting stations put out special programmes about the Choir and many of the girls gave individual interviews on both radio and TV. Stores were selling the records and many held autograph signing sessions in their music departments. The Choir performed at the Capitol Theatre which held over 3,000 people and they sang to packed and enthusiastic audiences during 10 days which far exceeded all expectations.

Many former Luton friends came back stage to say how proud they were of the girls. One of these, a Mr Horley Derbyshire, was a previous employee of R.Colin

Large Ltd. and he thought a journey of 130 miles was well worth it to hear the Choir sing. Also while in Sydney each of the girls received a surprise bouquet from an associate company of Laporte chemicals.

The girls were billeted all over Sydney with members of the Crusader Choir; some were on the other side of the Harbour Bridge and distances were quite considerable. The girls often had to find their own way home at night after concerts, something which certainly would not be allowed today.

Ten of the senior girls stayed in a residential centre normally used by Young Methodists attending conferences and they had to get used to prayer sessions which they found rather strange. The girls slept in bunks and one day came face to face with one of Australia's less welcome sights, a tarantula spider.

Two of the girls were asked to sing at a church service which was being broadcast and one of them actually turned up in shorts, thinking it was in a recording studio.

Free time was spent enjoying Sydney and its surrounds. Some of the girls were taken by members of the Victoria League to the Blue Mountains at Katoomba while others enjoyed a sail round the harbour. There was a barbecue lunch on the beach at Castle Rock Bay where they were guests of the Royal Motor Yacht Club; 75 lbs of meat disappeared in no time. Winifred Attwell attended one of the concerts and invited the girls to use her house on Bilgowlah beach for changing into their swim wear.

While the choir were in New South Wales they visited Wollongong and also had three days in Newcastle. Here they were met at the railway station by an army cadet band which then headed the procession of Vauxhall cars, in which the girls were travelling, all the way to the city hall while the crowd cheered and waved. Hospitality was provided by the Hamilton Rotary Club and a lunch at Lake Macquarie was hosted by the Victoria League.

The choir gave three concerts and the critics were again mixed. One said the choir as a whole were good but the soloists, although extremely pleasant, were in the main unspectacular. He did think the audience appreciated the girls singing whatever they sang.

From Newcastle it was back to Sydney on the night sleeper train but not much sleep for the girls as the train spent a long while in the sidings before leaving at 2.30am.

The plane taking the Choir to New Zealand was delayed by 15 minutes as six tearful girls took leave of their new found Australian boy friends.

During their New Zealand tour the girls travelled by coach and as the population in the towns was quite small they had to visit a lot of places. They were constantly on the move and were quite tired at the end of their trip. Naturally their hosts also wanted to take them out and about.

After one night at Christchurch they moved on the Thursday to Dunedin, known as the Edinburgh of New Zealand. It was here that the youngest member of the party, Maureen Beck, celebrated her 15th birthday and admitted to feeling a little homesick. In Dunedin Peggy Coggins stayed with a Jewish family as she had swapped with one of the girls who did not want to be billeted on her own. Peggy received a rather strange compliment from the family's 21 year old son who escorted her to the concert hall. "Every night I go to the concert hall and see all those beautiful girls and we have the old one. But I would not change her". Peggy did enjoy staying with them but was in disgrace for arriving home late on the first night. There was a performance of "Anastasia" at the theatre and one of the leads from the Luton performance of "Merrie England" in 1953 was in the play. Peggy, Mr and Mrs Davies, the tour manager and the star went back to the hotel afterwards and it got very late. The actor took Peggy back to her digs in a converted ambulance. She did not have a key and when she knocked on the door, a window opened and a voice said "Key's under the mat".

There were two concerts and then on Wednesday 29th Sept. they were in Invercargill, the most southerly part of the tour. The Choir's buses arrived in front of the Regent Theatre to be met by the familiar large crowds. Somebody called out "sing for us" so Mr Davies led the girls into the theatre foyer where they grouped themselves on the stairs and sang "The Lark in the Clear Air" and "The Happy Wanderer". They later gave two evening performances and a matinee. All were sold out and as a concession people were allowed to sit on the stairs of the dress circle. One girl's memory was of a visit to the dentist as she had an abscess on one of her teeth.

In typical fashion England was enjoying an Indian summer while the weather in New Zealand left a little to be desired. At Invercargill it was very cold and in one theatre it was so draughty that the pages of the music on the piano just blew over of their own accord. People did appreciate the Choir and when the coaches left town the hosts and crowds of well wishers sang "Auld Lang Syne" as the girls departed.

On the Friday they were back in Dunedin where they sang to an audience of 3,000 who did not want to leave. After 3 or 4 curtain calls Mr Davies returned to the stage and tried to lull them into feeling tired with "The Shepherd's Cradle Song". Peggy stayed with the Jewish family again and was able to attend their New Year celebrations before dashing off to the concert.

One young girl, Philippa Lousley, had her own private concert from some of the Choir who were visiting Wakari children's hospital. She had a ticket for their concert but had fallen from her bicycle and was taken to hospital instead. As the girls sang for her, patients and nurses from the other wards came to listen.

Once again girls employed at Vauxhall Motors and Electrolux were entertained by people from the sister companies in New Zealand.

After a one night stop in Timaru the girls had what Mr Davies called a "Kerridge sweetener." A memorable weekend in the Hermitage Lodge at the foot of Mount Cook in the Southern Alps. They were unfortunately confined to the hotel as a blizzard curtailed their sightseeing.

Choir girls advertising a Vauxhall car in New Zealand. Photo Chartres and Guthie (New Zealand).

This trip was followed by four nights in Christchurch with an autograph signing session at Hays stores in between concerts. From Christchurch they flew to Wellington in the North Island. Here they were given a Civic Reception by the Lord Mayor Mr Kitts. The Prime Minister, Mr Nash and the leader of the opposition were also there, the Prime Minister saying "From what I hear, the visit of these young ladies from England may prove to be the greatest achievement of the century in the promotion of friendship between our two countries".

The arrival of mail was always eagerly awaited and at Wellington there was a large amount. The girls got to hear about this and as Mr Davies had stipulated that letters were not to be distributed until after a performance, the girls thought they would shorten the concert by speeding up the singing. Mr Davies realised what was happening and announced to the audience "Well, it looks as if we have time for another number." The girls were beaten and did not try that one again.

Another 21st birthday was celebrated at an evening concert and a cake with candles on was carried on stage for Barbara Oakley. She made a brave attempt to blow out the candles.

While en route for Palmerston, at a lunch stop, the choir met up with the "Howard Morrison Quartet", a group of Maori singers. Many photographs were taken and the Maoris and girls sang together. The Choir were already well known in Palmerston North thanks to Mr William Sexton, the man who had been corresponding with the Luton lady who had put her address in the band of a hat sent for export. They had been writing to each other for some time and Mr Sexton had been broadcasting programmes about Luton and its Choir. He was pleased at last to be able to see and hear them in his own town.

On Mount Cook in the Snowy Mountains, New Zealand. Photo from Library Collection.

The weather had not really improved and in New Plymouth the concert was cut short. The girls were singing in the open air theatre at Brooklands Bowl, which was a beautiful setting with the stage surrounded by a lake. Unfortunately in early spring the temperature was not quite 40 degrees and there was a gale blowing, so the girls wore top coats and many had hot water bottles tucked inside their clothes. Over 2,000 people braved the cold to listen; they too had hot water bottles and were also wrapped in blankets. The Mayor eventually took pity on the girls and asked for the concert to be curtailed but many of the girls caught colds from that night.

In Hamilton the choir sang in the new 4,000 seater assembly hall of the Mormon college. Very strikingly set on the city's highest peak with the illuminated Temple against a dark sky.

The Choir had another chance to sing with the Maoris when they visited the thermal region of Rotorua and the native village of Whakarewarewa. Here they were shown round by Maoris including Rangi the chief guide. They were then entertained by women in traditional costumes giving demonstrations of dancing and swinging pois. The Choir sang for the Maori women and then the two groups joined to sing "Now is the Hour", singing the Maori words which the Luton girls had learnt especially for the tour.

It was just outside Auckland that the sponsor of the Kiwi Tour, Mr R.J.Kerridge, thanked the girls personally for their work on the tour. He was waiting in his Rolls Royce at a pre-arranged spot and actually came onto the coach to meet the girls and thank them for their efforts. Later each girl received a 21b box of "Winning Post" chocolates and £5 and they were also given vouchers for free entry to the Kerridge Odeons and to the gourmet restaurant. Mr and Mrs Davies, Peggy and the tour manager were invited to lunch at his home.

In Auckland itself a fleet of 15 cars ferried the girls to a buffet luncheon before rehearsals. There was a welcome from W.W.King, the general manager of Tappenden Motors and the president of the Millinery Promotion Committee, Mr E.T. Allen, presented Mrs Davies with a huge floral picture hat, the size of a bicycle wheel. It was made entirely of tulip petals and was a gesture to the world wide bond between the hat trade.

An unusual stage for one Choir performance was an escalator in a departmental store; luckily it was stationary as they stood on it to sing for the crowds. At the end of the tour, Mr Kerridge, who very seldom attended concerts, actually took his wife and family to two given by the Choir and all the family went to the airport to bid farewell to the girls. Mr N.J. Glover, Associate General Manager of Kerridge Odeon, also showed his appreciation in a letter sent to the Choir in which he said "The magnificent singing, the friendly disposition and the wonderful co-operation has left us with very happy memories of the Choir's visit to New Zealand and we trust that you will always look back with pleasure and satisfaction on your extremely successful tour of the Dominion."

The Choir flew back to Australia, touching down at Sydney before flying on to Melbourne. Many of their former hosts came to say hello again, and one girl had a surprise meeting with her brother who was in the Merchant Navy, his ship had docked just prior to her arrival.

The flight was late arriving at Sydney which then made it even later at Melbourne but this did not deter the young autograph hunters who mobbed the girls as they arrived at the terminal. In Melbourne they met with another emigrant, Janet Feasey, who had actually helped in England with the fitting of the tour outfits. She then emigrated with her husband to Australia and was waiting at Melbourne airport when the Choir landed. There were the usual parades, this time the Sunshine City Band and the Victoria Marching Association and the Choir sang the "Happy Wanderer". Amongst the 3,000 crowd were two original Choir members who were pleased to renew acquaintances. The Choir had a police escort as their fleet of Vauxhall cars took them to the city centre.

They gave four performances in a building used normally for boxing promotions and renamed The Festival Hall in their honour. It was in this hall that the second serious mishap befell another of the girls when June Ekins fell off the stage and cut her head rather badly. Peggy Coggins had to take her to the first aid attendant on duty and was asked to thread the needle so that he could stitch up the wound. When finished he said "Not bad for an old horse doctor".

While in Melbourne two of the girls became friendly with two determined young men. When the choir departed for Adelaide and flew the 600 miles, the two lads followed them the hard way, by road in an old Singer car. The boys were able to stay for several days with friends of the girl's host families before finally having to say "Goodbye".

The charity supported in Adelaide was the Central Methodist Mission and although six performances had been planned there was a great demand for tickets, so the Choir stayed an extra night to fit in another concert. Their hour and a half broadcast was from the Maughan Methodist Church in the "Pleasant Sunday Afternoon" series where Mr Davies gave an account of how the Choir began, then Maureen Rennie and Gayda Davison described what the Choir meant to them. After the programme the Director of the City Radio and Television Corporation presented Mr Davies with a complete recording of the proceedings. On the following Thursday they had a quarter of an hour slot during the opening of Channel 7 TV station.

The last stop on this fantastic tour was in Perth. Attendance at concerts in both Adelaide and Perth were sell outs, a record as the venues were both large and expensive, with tickets prices ranging from 10/- to 30/- (50p to £1.50).

The final concert was very emotional, the audience sang "Will Ye N'er Come Back Again?" and threw streamers and the Choir responded with "Land of Hope and Glory". The soloists and Music Librarian were introduced to the audience and Anne Norcross remembers standing on the stage with tears running down her face. A fantastic climax to a tremendous tour.

Broadcasting in Adelaide. Photo from Library Collection.

Four days of well earned rest at Forest House followed, the girls lazing on the beach getting sunburnt. As the weather got warmer, the girls found it very strange to see the shops decorated for Christmas and the traditional figure of Father Christmas with his fur trimmings, while they were in summer dresses.

The journey home was via the Cocos Islands and Colombo with a 24 hour stop at the Mount Lavinia Hotel in Ceylon (Sri Lanka). Mr Davies had always threatened the girls that if any of them misbehaved they would be put on the next plane home. 12 of the girls decided that as they were going home anyway they would accept the KLM crew's invitation to join them at the "Little Hut", a night club in the grounds. They joined up with a Lufthansa crew and one from BOAC and had a great evening. It ended with them all singing carols from different countries, although the KLM crew's contribution was "Tulips from Amsterdam". The girls described it as "A great end to a fantastic time".

Amongst the wonderful memories of the tour were the contrasts of lifestyles. One thing that surprised the girls was the lack of indoor sanitation. A bathroom and shower were considered an absolute necessity but in many cases houses could not boast of all mod cons. Many times as the plane was coming in to land at various towns and cities the girls would look out of the window and mutter "sentry boxes in the garden again". Their way of referring to the outside toilets.

Food was also different, as the Australians had a stewed breakfast of meat and thick gravy or chops. However the quantities of fresh vegetables like asparagus and fresh tropical fruit such as paw - paw, passion fruits, custard apples and pineapple was delightful. One thing was the same as home; no matter what time the girls arrived home from a concert, the kettle and grill would go on for tea and toast.

The Australian styles of architecture, illustrated by the beautiful houses in Sydney and Perth, impressed the girls. The majority of houses were single storey and in Queensland many of them were wooden and built on stilts. The utility room containing a washing machine, spin dryer and a stone sink was a novelty. The sinks looked like old fashion horse troughs and at first the girls feared for their nylon undies when they did their washing.

The other major difference was distance - residential areas being a long way from the city centres, 45 minutes journey on a rattling tram was a normal experience. Cars were used to ferry the girls around most of the time but if the host was not available, the girls had to find their own way.

It was dark when the Choir returned to Luton. The Town Hall was flood lit, the municipal flag and the Union Jack were flying. Several hundred people, including the parents who had not been able to get to the airport, lined the streets and the Mayor, Ald. Mrs Andrews waited on the Town Hall steps. As the coaches arrived the girls were singing "Waltzing Matilda". They dismounted and joined the Mayor in singing "The Happy Wanderer" before going with their parents to Dunstable Road school to collect their luggage.

Later at the Christmas Buffet dance, organised at the George Hotel by the Parents and Supporters Association, Mrs Davies was presented with a coffee set for looking after the girls so well. Peggy Coggins received a marcasite brooch for her work on the tour and Pat Corley was presented with a compact for deputising for Peggy. The Olivestone Cup for that year went to Beryl Anstee who had not been able to go on tour because of ill health but had kept the remainder of the Choir together while the others were in Australasia. Mr Glaister Newton had come to Luton each week to take the rehearsals.

Mr Davies receiving the Illuminated Address from the Mayor when the Choir returned from Australasia. Photo Luton News.

There was an official reception at the Town Hall on Thursday 17th December, first in the main committee rooms where at a buffet tea the girls met the Councillors and were presented to the Mayor. Everybody then went into the council chamber where the Mayor presented an illuminated address, with the Corporation seal affixed, to Mr Davies. Each of the 47 girls received a photographic copy. It read: *"The Mayor, Aldermen and Councillors of the Borough of Luton extend their warmest congratulations to the members of the Luton Girls Choir and their Musical Director Mr Arthur Davies MBE on the outstanding success of their recent concert tour of Australia and New Zealand.*

The excellence of their performance and conduct abroad, besides bringing credit to themselves and their native town, did much to maintain good relations between the Commonwealth Countries and the Mother Country."

The Choir then sang "Lark in the Clear Air" and "The Happy Wanderer" and Julie Barrett gave a vote of thanks.

The tour cost £71,000; it only made a profit of about £5,000 and the sponsors said the profit did not match the time and effort spent in arrangements. In every other way however everybody agreed it had been a great success. The girls were praised for their behaviour and deemed good ambassadors for both Luton and England. The "Luton News" received many letters from people in Australia saying how much they had appreciated the Choir's visit.

Eight years later in Western Australia the TV stations were still showing the Luton Girls Choir Tour as they had done each Christmas before, in answer to public demand. Even today Australians make enquiries about the Choir and are sad it no longer exists.

After Australasia.

After their successful tour of Australasia there was some talk of the Choir going to South Africa. At the time feelings were very strong regarding apartheid so it was decided not to make the visit.

The Choir continued to give concerts around the country during the first part of 1960. In Bournemouth that year there was trouble with the local youth trying to get into the hotel using ladders at the windows. The proprietors were not amused and the Choir were asked not to use that hotel again.

In June the Skefko Ball Bearing Co Ltd. celebrated 50 years of being in Luton, giving two Jubilee concerts at the Savoy cinema. The Choir, with the Band of the Irish Guards, sang at both performances before the showing of the film "Carry on Nurse". Skefko had invited various Luton groups to share in the celebrations and at the afternoon concert were the firm's pensioners, transport authorities, pupils from Luton High School and Luton College of Technology. In the evening, the Mayor and Mayoress, together with guests from the Luton and Dunstable Hospital, the Post Office telephone staff and the police, enjoyed the show.

In November at the Luton College of Technology the Choir had what was described as a "Family Night for the Choir". The first large scale concert in Luton since the Australasian tour, it was a night for family, friends and former members, the latter being given a box of chocolates as a memento when they arrived. On the front of the programme was a picture of the Choir, this time in groups not in the usual straight lines.

Julie Barrett introduced Mr Davies as "at the piano we have your good friend and mine with a little more weight and a little less hair, but still the same". Mr Davies talked about "My friends in blue" and during the interval all former members, including the Choir's first secretary, queued up to meet him. Later they all joined in singing "Someday We Shall Meet Again". That evening was a foretaste of things to come. On the back of the programme was a note saying the following year was the Choir's Silver Jubilee Year. Details of former members were required so they could all be contacted and help to celebrate the great occasion.

Chapter Twelve

The Silver Jubilee

By 1961 there were probably only six national choirs still singing from about twenty six in 1953. Luton's was still going strong and January saw the Choir again in their home town, this time at the Skefko Social Centre in Sundon, in aid of the Sundon Church hall. Mr Davies had been asked to include as many favourites as possible to please the audience of family and friends. Items ranged from "Little Donkey" to songs from grand opera with Scottish and Spanish dancers doing their bit. The "echo" effect was also included.

In February there was a problem at Wolverton again when the Choir were left in the dark. The lights went off during the concert but the soloist bravely carried on and then the Choir grouped themselves round the piano and sang by torch light. The Chief Constable was in the audience and hastily sent for floodlights but the hall lights eventually came on again.

In April the Choir had an unusual request when a lady asked them to sing at a concert in memory of her mother who had died the previous year. A programme of sacred music was sung in the London City Road Wesley Chapel.

That month there was a link with their past when the Choir were asked to sing at Luton King Street Congregational Church. This was to celebrate the 21st year of Luton and District Sunday School Union Eisteddfod. It had all begun in 1932 but there had been a break during the war and also in 1953.

The seaside concerts were still well attended. At Bournemouth the Choir shared the same programme as Rawicz and Landauer and it was Barbara Chance's last concert; she was singing as a soloist. She had joined the Choir in 1947 and had sung in 1,600 concerts and attended 2,300 rehearsals. She had been to Scandinavia, Australia and New Zealand but thought her most memorable event had been when the Choir sang in St Paul's Cathedral. On the Sunday the soloist was 13 year old Theresa Burnham. There was a full house and people were even sitting on the side of the stage. Theresa's singing was so well received, that although it was not normally encouraged, she had to give an encore.

At Worthing in September the Corporation gave Mr and Mrs Davies a box of chocolates to celebrate their wedding anniversary.

The main event of the year however was in November, marking the Choir's quarter of a century. Twenty five years of singing were celebrated with three massive concerts, Luton Council contributing £150 towards the celebrations. A silver covered brochure entitled "Story of the Luton Girls Choir" was produced. This history of the Choir's achievements was written by Hedley Gore and there were tributes from many stars and eminent people, both local and national. These included the Rt. Hon. Charles Hill, Dorothy Seddon (Matron of the Luton and Dunstable Hospital), Ronald Waldman, Eric Robinson, the Prime Minister of New Zealand, Keith Holyoak, the Governor of Queensland, Henry Abel Smith and the Rt Hon. the Lord Mayor of Sydney, Alderman H.F. Jensen. The brochure was full of adverts from prominent local films which also helped towards the cost.

The three concerts took place in the Luton College of Technology on Monday 6th, Wednesday 15th and Thursday 23rd of November and each was a sell out. There was a different guest artiste each evening and a complete change of programme, a tremendous effort in just one month. The commere for all three concerts was Julie Barrett.

The first concert started with the Choir's song "Music in my Heart". This was followed by a selection from the songs sung by the Choir through the years. 1936 - 41 including "March of the Grenadiers" and a solo "Like to a Damask Rose". 1942 - 48 was music from films and opera with "Musetta's Waltz Song" from "La Boheme and "Habanera" from Carmen. Two members of the Choir, dressed in Spanish costume and clicking castanets, appeared from the back of the hall. Monday's guest artistes were Rawicz and Landauer who played a selection of tunes including "Exodus" and then accompanied the Choir in the finale to the first half as they sang a selection from "Glamorous Night". During the interval Mr Davies presented the Mayor with a copy of the Jubilee Book.

The second half opened with the girls singing "Oh Deah What Ken the Mattah Be" from "Fantasy of Nursery Rhymes"; this had been a great favourite of the Australasian tour. The 1954 - 60 section also included "My Heart and I" in memory of Richard Tauber. Rawicz and Landauer then played "Merrie England Dances", "Invitation to the Dance" and "Orpheus in the Underworld". This was not enough for the audience and after three curtain calls the couple then played the "Ritual Fire Dance".

In the 1961 section Choir and pianists again joined together for a selection of songs from "South Pacific" followed by the "Blue Danube".

After three hours of music, former Choir members joined the present Choir on the stage to sing "Someday We Shall Meet Again".

On Wednesday 15th the guest artistes were members of the Band of the Irish Guards. The commere introduced Mr Davies and then Mr Alan Malden of the National Children's Home who spoke of the staggering £70,000 which the Choir had raised for charity, £20,000 of which had gone to the Homes.

The music started with "Britons Sing" and "Tales from the Vienna Woods". Teressa Burnham's solo "Bird Songs at Eventide" was followed by lively and quiet tunes played by the Irish Guards, including both a trumpet and trombone solo. The Australian section featured two pieces, again especially arranged for the Choir,

With Rawicz and Landauer at the first Silver Jubilee Concert. Photo Luton News.

"The Alexandra Waltz" and "Waltzing Matilda". The "Nun's Chorus" by Strauss and the "Gypsy Chorus" by Bizet brought the first half to a close.

The Irish Band started the second half and then Mr Davies played "Forgotten Dreams" on the piano, accompanied by a section of the Choir. The girls then performed their "echoing trick" in the "Snowy Snowy Mountains". The band played again and after more solos the Choir sang "A Romberg Rendezvous" especially for Glaister Newton who had written the arrangement. Mr Newton was in the audience and stood for a well deserved round of applause.

The pianist Semprini was the guest star on Thursday 23rd November. The evening opened with the "Tritsch Tratsch Polka" and the first half also included "Break of Day" and "Count Your Blessings". "The Happy Wanderer" typified the Choir as Luton's ambassadors of song and there was a last minute inclusion, by popular demand, of "We'll Gather Lilacs". Semprini then played a selection with a classical flavour.

Just before the interval Mr Davies was presented with a bound volume containing press cuttings and photographs, compiled by New Zealand's Palmerston North Junior Chamber of Commerce, as a memento of the Choir's tour in 1959.

During the second half of the concert the audience joined in as Semprini played a collection of old favourites, "My Blue Heaven" and "The Cloud with the Silver Lining".

An encore produced "Around the World", "Among my Souvenirs" and "California Here I Come". Again a combined effort of pianist and audience. The Choir gave the first public performance of "Automne", a new vocal arrangement by Glaister Newton, and the concert ended with the past and present members of the Choir on stage singing "The Holy City".

After the former members had left the stage, one of the senior members, Pat Willis, paid tribute to Mrs Davies as "The one who is always with us wherever we go" and presented her with a silver vase on behalf of the Choir. Meryl Craven then added a bouquet of flowers.

During the three concerts 18 soloists had taken part and for some it was their first public solo. Former members of the Choir who were in the audience again received a box of chocolates as a memento of the evening.

To end their Silver Jubilee Year there was a Thanksgiving Recital in Luton Parish Church on Sunday December 3rd 1961. The Rev Harold Frankham, Vicar of Luton, officiated and George Thalben Ball was at the organ.

During December the long time Choir follower, Mr John Watson of St Albans, presented Mr Davies with an illuminated scroll. The scroll was headed: *Tribute to the creator of the Luton Girls Choir on its Silver Jubilee Year 1936 - 1961. To you Arthur Davies MBE founder and sole musical director, tutor, conductor and pianist of this world renowned Choir, whose Silver Jubilee you now celebrate, I tender my sincere congratulations and gratitude for this wonder of amateur achievements . . .*

Singing at one of the Silver Jubilee Concerts. Photo Luton News.

Mr Watson had been a long standing fan of the Choir, travelling to their concerts in England and even following them to Australia. He said he had prepared the scroll because no such testimonial had come from any other source and it was high time it did.

His sentiments were echoed by the Choir and many people in the town. For 25 years Mr Davies had publicised Luton throughout the world and the town did not give him any Civic recognition.

Chapter Thirteen

This is Your Life

The greatest public accolade for Arthur Davies was when he featured as "the subject" in the TV programme "This is your Life". Peggy Coggins had asked Ronnie Waldman if Mr Davies could be considered for the programme during the Choir's Jubilee year. Ronnie Waldman said he would be in America but would look into it. The programme actually took place on Monday 29th January 1962.

Eamon Andrews presenting Arthur Davies with the "Red Book". Photo BBC.

Mr Davies hailed Peggy in the street and told her the BBC had been trying to get in contact with her. This began a series of secret calls and meetings, as she obviously could not speak to them from the office in case she was overheard. Peggy told Mr Davies that the BBC wanted the Choir to record a Spring performance. He was not very keen, thinking it would mean a lot of work for the Choir but she persuaded him to agree. He said if she could arrange for the girls to have a day off work then she could go ahead.

The Red Lion Hotel was the venue for meetings between Peggy and the research team. She gave them all the information on Mr Davies but it was she who had to do a lot of the organising, like agreeing the music with Rawicz and Landauer and Major Jaeger of the Irish Guards, as well as contacting all the firms for the girls to have time off.

The great day arrived and the girls were all very excited; some had not been to the studios before. They were not told that it was a "This is your Life" programme but there was much speculation. Mrs Davies, who did not normally attend TV appearances, was taken to London independently by Peggy's cousin. Plans also had to be made to occupy Mr Davies for the afternoon while the Choir and guests rehearsed. Arrangements were made for him to spend the time with his friends, the Harper Smiths. They were great fans of the Choir and always attended the Watford concerts; the girls had also sung at some of their private functions.

The Choir arrived at the studio, began rehearsing for the supposed concert and then Eamon Andrews walked in and sprang his surprise. Mr Davies was whisked away to his friends while taxis carrying various guests did circuits of the studio until he had disappeared.

Preparations were going on in the studio throughout the afternoon. The Choir rehearsed from 2.00 to 2.15pm and there was a walk through with the cast from 2.30 to 3.00pm. The Choir then went for a rehearsal in St Michael's Hall until 4.00pm while the Irish Guards rehearsed in the studio until 3.45pm. The first rehearsal for the whole company was 4.15 to 5.00pm followed by a second one 5.15 to 6.00pm. The show then went out live between 7.30 and 8.00pm.

The programme started with a shot of Mr Davies rehearsing the Choir, enter Eamon Andrews who announced "The man who has brought entertainment to millions of people - the man who founded a Choir which is now a national institution - the man who has never sought the limelight, Arthur Davies MBE This is Your Life". The lights went up slowly on a gauze, revealing the Choir singing "My Heart and I" as Eamon Andrews welcomed Mr Davies. At the end of the song the lights faded and the tabs closed.

There had been a hitch when Mr Davies's old music teacher, Mrs Guest-Hubbard, had refused to come to the studios. As Miss Lilla Morris she had given piano lessons to an eight year old Arthur Davies and was supposed to tell the story of how he had been singing a duet at a concert with one of her little girl pupils. Arthur got carried away and pushed the little girl off the stage. At the last minute the elderly lady refused to appear, so Eamon Andrews started the show by stating that Mr Davies did not favour any girl over another but one girl chose him for a very important role. In 1940 when Mr Davies answered a knock at his door he found a thirteen year old war evacuee standing outside. She said "If you don't mind Mr Davies I would like to come and live with you". The girl's name was Anne Henry and she lived with the Davies' until she got married in 1951, going then to live in Salisbury, Rhodesia. Of course she had been flown back for the programme and there was a joyful reunion.

Next came the sound of a solo cornet and hundreds of Lutonians watching knew that meant Harry Mortimer OBE. Together as boyhood friends from about 9 or 10 years old they had given many concerts in Luton, Harry Mortimer playing the cornet and Arthur Davies singing and playing the piano.

Eamon Andrews then talked about Mr Davies' training and how he became conductor of the largest Church Choir in Luton. He recounted the story of the Wolverton concert where the door was locked and there was no piano, before Margaret Goodman - the Choir's first secretary - told how all 30 members of the Choir would meet in her parent's house to rehearse before their concerts. In those days they would give concerts anywhere they could get an audience.

Ronnie Waldman, a friend of the Choir's since the '40s, remembered the Richard Tauber episode, when Tauber refused at first to sing with "a bunch of amateurs" but changed his mind after listening to the girls at a rehearsal.

When Eamon Andrews talked about the Choir touring both at home and abroad, pictures were shown of the girls on board ship and when they were flying. He then went on to talk about famous people the Choir had met and suggested Mr Davies sometimes made unusual demands of them. Two voices were heard off stage saying "For the Luton Girls Choir we will do anything". The voices belonged of course to the two famous musicians Rawicz and Landauer. They had lost count of how many times they had appeared with the Choir; it had started in 1949 and the last time had been the previous year when they helped the Choir celebrate its 25th anniversary. The pianists made it a rule never to accompany singers but even this was broken during the anniversary - for Arthur. The rule was then broken again as they accompanied the Choir in a shortened version of Mr Davies's own composition, "My Heart is Singing".

Eamon Andrews then talked about the number of times the Choir had sung in front of Royalty, first in the Command performance for King George VI and Queen Elizabeth and then later at concerts attended by Princess Elizabeth and Princess Margaret. This, he said, must have set the seal of approval on the choir, banishing the days of trundling around borrowed pianos. Cue for the appearance of Miss Dorothy Seddon, Matron of the Luton and Dunstable Hospital. She said the Choir were still often borrowing pianos and trundling them around. When they made their annual Christmas Morning visit to the Hospital to sing carols to the patients, the piano which had been borrowed from the doctors' flats, was moved from ward to ward.

Mrs Davies then recalled her duties as chaperone and universal aunt to the girls. Her happiest memory was of accompanying Mr Davies to Buckingham Palace to receive his MBE.

It was then the turn of that joker, Major Jaeger. As he came onto the stage he muttered to Mr Davies, "Arthur, your flies are undone". The Guards and the Choir had appeared together many times and Major Jaeger was convinced it was Arthur who had pushed him in the lake during the "Merrie England " pageant at Luton Hoo. The path to the orchestra pit was very close to the water and "Mr Davies was right behind me" said Major Jaeger accusingly. '1 suddenly found myself up to my knees in it". The Major said the Guards and the Choir were linked in "Holy wedlock", this being the introduction for Bob and Marion Oades, a Guardsman and

Arthur Davies, Choir and friends in This is Your Life. Photo BBC.

Arthur and Gwen Davies and friends at the end of This is Your Life*. Photo BBC.*

a Choir girl whose engagement had been announced at a Royal Festival Hall performance. They had subsequently married and later gone to live in Canada. They too had been flown over to appear that evening.

To finish the evening Bob joined the Band and Marion joined the Choir to sing a final tribute to Mr Davies. After the broadcast there was a party in the TV centre and a chance for all who had taken part, except the Choir and the Band, to see a recording of the show. Mr Davies made a speech thanking all the participants. The girls had to go home on their coach immediately after the show, escorted by Mr Arthur Taylor, one of Mr Davies' friends.

The "Red Book", with all the photographs, was later sent to Mr Davies who had enjoyed every minute of his evening. At that time it had been one of the most expensive shows of the series to stage because of the numbers involved. Mr Davies asked Peggy Coggins why she had not been included in the show. She told him secretaries were not considered newsworthy enough. He had introduced her as his secretary to Eamon Andrews who replied "Yes 1 know, she has done a lot for the show". On her copy of the script Eamon Andrews wrote "to the girl who made it all possible" and Peggy still treasures it to this day. The next day his house and office were flooded with messages, phone calls and telegrams of congratulations from his many friends and associates.

Chapter Fourteen

The Sixties and Seventies

After the excitement of the Jubilee Concerts and Mr Davies' "This is your Life" programme, the Choir settled down to their normal round of concerts. In February they again joined forces with a Northern Choir, this time the Wheatsheaf Girls Choir from Doncaster. Thirty girls in cream blouses and tan skirts joined the blue clad girls at the Luton College of Technology in a programme, "Songs for Saturday Night". The northern musical director was Mr John Barker and the Choir had also sung abroad, twice in France and twice in Northern Ireland. The northern girls stayed with their Luton counterparts while down south.

At the end of April the Luton girls made the trip north to Doncaster for another "Songs for Saturday Night" concert. Both Choirs were entertained to tea in the Spring Gardens by the Doncaster Co-operative Society and later at the concert the Luton girls were welcomed to Doncaster by the Mayor. Their accommodation in turn was provided by members of the Doncaster Choir.

On Easter Monday the Choir were seen on TV. The pre-recorded programme, with its cast of 325, included the Band of the Irish Guards and Michael Freeman and his Ladies Orchestra, the soloist being Margot Barry. The highlight of the Choir's 16 minute contribution was their backing of the soloist in the Nuns' Chorus; 20 girls were dressed as nuns and carried lighted candles. The robes were borrowed from a local church but their wimples had been made by Peggy Coggins who had to check with the wardrobe department to make sure they looked authentic. The Choir also sang "Finlandia" backed by 166 musicians. Most reviewers said the screen looked far too crowded. Mr Davies said TV shows were exacting, complicated and tiring, while the girls had to have lots of patience. Professional artistes could adapt to TV work but amateurs found it exhausting.

At Whitsun the Choir appeared at the Cardigan Eisteddfod. 63 girls made the Choir's first visit to West Wales, receiving a civic welcome from Mr Ivor Radley the Mayor of Cardigan and being entertained to supper at the Guildhall by the Ladies Committee. During the weekend the girls stayed with local families, sight-seeing tours occupying their spare time. The organisers paid the Choir's expenses of about £250 and the girls sang at the opening concert. Mr Davies told them it was a great honour as only the top people were invited to appear. They were on stage for about two and a half hours singing 16 of the 40 songs originally submitted for selection by Mr Davies. There was a mixture of songs, not just classical items, and they also bravely sang the hymn "Sanctus" in Welsh. One of the girl's parents helped them with the pronunciation.

Appearing with the Choir were two members of the Sadler's Wells Opera Company, Ronald Dowd a tenor, and Raymond Herincx, baritone. The singing was amplifed through speakers and could be heard up and down the Teify Valley. The girls were told the event drew a larger audience than it had the previous year and the local chapel even started its service 15 minutes early, so that people did not have to rush to get to the concert.

Luton was honoured by a visit to the town of her Majesty Queen Elizabeth on Friday November 2nd 1962 when, together with Prince Philip, she came to open the new Central Library. Sixty girls, who had joined the Choir before 1961, took part in the day's entertainment by giving a 20 minute concert in the Library theatre to the Royal visitors, local dignitaries and some lucky parents of the library staff.

The programme was approved by the Queen's equerry but Mrs Davies was worried about the girls singing the word "bellies", during the song from "Carousel", in front of Royalty. There were lots of jokey articles in the national press but the girls sang "we are so full" instead of using the offending word. The girls felt rather silly about the whole affair and Prince Philip had obviously read about the fuss because he sported a large grin as the song was sung.

The girls were instructed to keep their eyes on Mr Davies but human nature won and many sly glances were directed at the front row. The concert was introduced very professionally by a nervous Julie Barrett and the Choir sang "Elizabeth of England" by Haydn Wood. This was followed by "Music in My Heart", the "Blue Bird" by C.V. Stanford and then that song from "Carousel". Patricia Patterson and Breada Barry were the highland dancers in the "Keel Row". The concert ended with "Someday we Shall Meet Again".

Prince Philip then chatted for a few minutes to Mr Davies asking him if the girls wearing kilts were the ones who played the pipes ie. The Dagenham Girl Pipers. He also asked Mr Davies how he found the girls to sing in the Choir, did he advertise? Mr Davies said he had a waiting list.

Julie Barrett and the dancers were also lucky enough to be presented to the Queen and Prince Philip and to actually say a few words to them. This was the fourth time Mr Davies had been presented to a reigning monarch, twice to King George V1 and twice to his daughter Queen Elizabeth.

January 1963 found the Choir singing in the dark, in Letchworth. This was due to a fuse blowing in one of the local sub-stations just before the concert and power was not restored for an hour and a quarter. Joking that he felt like Liberace, Mr Davies had six candles on his piano and the soloists sang from the pulpit by the light of just one. There were 400 people in the audience and Mr Davies did not want to let them down.

The weather was exceptionally cold that winter and the girls wore white woollen stoles over their dresses. Other local concerts also had their problems, with bad weather affecting audience attendance at Hoddesdon and making travel conditions hazardous when the Choir went to Tring.

At Easter the girls had a West coast tour with a trip to Devon. They sang in Exeter, Barnstaple, Tavistock and Plymouth. Leaving Luton on Good Friday their first performance was a sacred recital that evening at the Southernhay Congregational Church in Exeter. On Saturday they were in Plymouth and after sightseeing, lunch was provided by one of Plymouth's leading department stores; their concert that evening was in the Central Hall.

On Sunday the afternoon concert was in Barnstaple and was a special event to raise money for a church in Woolacombe. The Vicar had written to Mr Davies who suggested that he join forces with another fund raiser to help with expenses. From Bamstaple the girls travelled to Tavistock and on Sunday evening sang at the Town Hall.

The other three concerts were for the Derriford Church building fund and had been initiated by Mrs B.Flintoff, then one of the church Deacons but formerly of Luton where she had been accompanist for the Luton Choral Society. On the Monday when the girls returned to Luton from Plymouth they gave an impromptu rendering of the "Happy Wanderer" as they left the bus station.

In May and June there were two performances with Rawicz and Landauer. The first, a charity concert with various stars in aid of the Ealing and District Society for Mentally Handicapped Children, was a clash of cultures. The programme started with an "up and coming" rock band and as fans of this type of music could not afford the ticket prices, the audience greeted their efforts with stony silence and then perfunctory applause. The Choir fared much better when they produced a "musical tour" of Britain. Arranged by Walter Landauer, he had included traditional folk songs from all parts of the British Isles. In June, at the Winter Gardens in Bournemouth, the "musical tour" idea was used again.

Summer time saw the usual visits to Folkestone, Eastbourne and Worthing. It was the Choir's thirteenth trip to the latter and they were still able to pull in the people, their visit attracting the largest audience to the Pavilion that year.

At home in November the Choir had a shock when their concert at the Technical College was cancelled because of a by-election. The date had already been changed twice and Mr Davies said it was the first time he had been forced to cancel a performance. It was sad that it was in his home town.

In April 1964 Dunstable began a year of celebrations to commemorate the centenary of their Royal Charter. The Queensway Hall was opened, the first event being a concert by the Luton Girls Choir and the Band of the Irish Guards. This proved to be so popular that it was decided to have a repeat performance in

November. The best part of the programme was the combination of Choir and Band in the March and Chorus from "Carmen".

A full page advertisement for the concert, appearing in the Luton News in March, listed the Choir's impressive record to date. Over 1,000 concerts, 20 TV appearances and 53 broadcasts, £70,000 had been raised for charity and the Choir had sung in 300 towns and cities from Luton to Australia.

Perhaps a sign of how the times were changing, in the programme for the concert, as well as a list of Choir members there was an invitation to any girl wishing to join the Choir to ring the Choir office number.

Mr Davies' requirements were still the same. When interviewed before a concert in Eastbourne he was asked what he did in his spare time. He smiled and said he had little of it. "You can't get success without hard work. Even in these days of affluent society and easy influence the people who show up are the ones who work". His mental list of what he believed were the essentials of life were the courage and convictions even to the sacrifice of popularity and that any progress must be flavoured with hard work and candour.

Road travel was becoming difficult and in September the Choir were very late for one of their concerts in Croydon, the coaches being delayed by traffic. Luckily it was a combined effort with the Irish Guards who, with Major Jaeger, had to amuse the audience for an hour before the girls arrived.

The Choir was beginning to change during the late '60s in keeping with the general mood. It was no longer broadcasting and as it did not feature in the top musical entertainment of the age, was not making many records; some magazines had already written it off. There were, however, some girls who were actually pleased to be singing in a Choir still able to entertain audiences on a regular basis.

Nevertheless the girls were affected by the new fashions in hair styles, the wearing of jewellery and the modern outlook. It was harder for them to be 100% loyal to the Choir against the taunts of their friends and boyfriends and the latter were not so tolerant. Girls were not so inclined to attend all the rehearsals and there was a greater divergence on the musical scene. Mr Davies commented on the fact that very few homes now possessed a piano and the girls could not read music. Homes were no longer used to making their own entertainment.

In the early years of the Choir up to the middle 50's no girl dared look away from Mr Davies during a song as he would stop, start, speed along or drag slowly and quietly. To look up even briefly meant a girl would be hopelessly lost. In the later years, as an older man, he kept a strict tempo and some girls looked round, so a lot of the magic was lost. Nevertheless, most of the girls who were still singing were as dedicated as ever and later were very upset when former members criticised them in subsequent radio interviews.

Venues to accommodate a large choir were harder to find, costs were escalating and the demand for their type of music was diminishing. Mr Davies was also getting older and so the pace of the Choir gradually slowed down. The girls were still supporting the NCH with their weekend visits and appearing at the coast during the summer season but were less in demand for big musical spectaculars.

It was in support of the NCH in June 1966 that the Choir made their last big tour, a Whitsun weekend in Jersey. The Choir had no contacts on the island and when Peggy Coggins and an NCH fund organiser, Sister Judith Kerridge, went there in advance to make arrangements, they received very little help from the Methodist Church. The Minister said they would have to sing in the choir stalls in the gallery and this was not suitable. It was only when the church organist introduced them to Leslie Picot, a well known Jersey accountant, that things looked more hopeful.

He arranged for the Choir to sing in one of the country churches in Zion and also to appear in the Opera House. Mr Picot met the girls at the airport and after a photo call by the plane and lunch in the airport lounge they were taken on a tour of the island. The Rotary club entertained them to tea at The Good Companions Club and their first concert was that evening, Friday 2nd. The concert lasted for three and a half hours with a break for one of the NCH representatives to give a short talk on the work of the homes.

The second concert on the Saturday was again at the Opera House. His Excellency, the Lieut. Governor, Sir Michael Villiers and his wife were in the audience and Mr and Mrs Davies, Peggy Coggins and two of the senior Choir girls were presented to His Excellency after the show.

The farewell concert on Sunday was in the Zion Methodist Church after the evening service. Entitled "Music for Sunday" it included items by Handel, Schubert and Mendelssohn. There was only seating for 500 but the audience were obviously impressed as the collection of £117 was the largest ever received at a concert. It normally averaged around £50.

Throughout the weekend the Choir stayed with hosts in private houses; accompanying parents were in local hotels. The girls were entertained very well and on Saturday there was a lavish lunch at the biggest hotel, L'Horizon at St Brelade's Bay, in their honour.

A grant to the tour was made from the Choir's own funds so that all the cost did not have to come from profits made during the weekend.

In November the Choir had been singing for thirty years and of course this warranted a special celebration. The venue was Watford Town Hall and with the brass bands from GUS (Footwear) BMC and Luton conducted by their friend Harry Mortimer, the first "Gala Rhapsody" took place.

The show started with an off stage fanfare of trumpets then the girls took their places, followed by the bandsmen. The concert featured music from three decades of singing with such diverse songs as "Tales from the Vienna Woods" and excerpts from "South Pacific". There was also a first performance of "More than Love" a song based on Beethoven's "Sonata Pathetique".

The programme from the first Gala Rhapsody. Photo Bob Norman.

It was the number of former members who, when meeting Mr Davies in town, told him how much they missed singing with the Choir, that gave him the idea of a combined gathering of voices of the older girls singing with the present Choir. He decided to try and on that evening the former members joined the girls in singing "Count Your Blessings" and the "Easter Hymn" from Cavalleria Rusticana. As Mr Davies welcomed them he said they were his "thrill of a lifetime" and he had many blessings to count over the thirty years with the Choir. There was a grand finale with Elgar's "Pomp and Circumstance" for bands and Choir and then the audience joined them both for a hearty rendering of the chorus of "Land of Hope and Glory".

Presentations were made to Mr and Mrs Davies and former Choir girl Marie Robinson said as she presented Mrs Davies with a bouquet, "At the time we didn't realise what a sacrifice it was, but since we've married we've known what a lot of your husband's time you have missed and how much you've given yourself".
The pattern was set and the joining of present and former members became an annual event and the "Gala Chorus" also sang in other venues big enough to hold a large group. In a later radio interview some of the former members said how much they had enjoyed appearing again on the stage and receiving the applause; the thrill was still there.

In spite of the disappointing article in the Hereford Times saying hardly anyone under the age of 30 would listen to the Luton Girls Choir in preference to the Beatles, an audience of 500 people came to hear them on their first visit there in April 1967. The girls made the 250 mile round trip and sang to a full house, with extra seating needed. That same April an unusual engagement saw 39 of the girls singing at the 34th anniversary of Lullingstone Silk Farm. This was to bless the silk worms in the annual service following the traditional agricultural blessing ceremonies. This service was in the church of Ayot St Lawrence and as well as a small tray of silk worms staff took along their stock and equipment to be blessed. These included raw silk on a spindle, a small mulberry tree, a rearing tray, a basket of cocoons, a weaver's shuttle and a length of silk. At the end of the procession was an ecclesiastical stole of silk damask which was presented to the Rector, who wore it during the service.

In September the "Evening Post" featured a large picture of the Choir in 1948 and did a "where are they now?" article, producing memories from a lot of former members.

Another chance to swop memories came at a second "Gala Rhapsody" Concert in Watford on October 29th, when the same bands, with Harry Mortimer, joined the Choir and former members. The evening was also a time for present giving. On behalf of the Choir, the Luton Mayor, Alderman Frank Lester and Peggy Coggins gave Mr Davies a reel-to-reel tape recorder for his birthday. Earlier that night Mr Davies had presented a new cornet, bought by the Choir, to Mr Albert Coupe, musical director of the Luton Band. The Band had launched a fund for new instruments as those they were using were nearly 50 years old. This was their first piece of new equipment, suitably engraved so that the name of the Luton Girls Choir would be linked with that of the Luton Band.

In November 1967 Mr Davies arranged a Thanksgiving concert at the Luton Parish Church. He said that he had a lot to be grateful for with the Choir and his life of music so he presented a programme of religious music in aid of the Church restoration fund and the audience were also able to hear two organ solos by the Parish Church organist.

The younger ones still fell for the "old tricks". At Sandra Goodman's first concert at Luton's High Town Methodist Church, the Choir were singing "Down in the Forest" by Landon Ronald. The church was surrounded by trees and she thought the timing was wonderful when the birds whistled in the right places. It was some time before she realised the bird noises were being provided by Peggy Coggins on her whistle.

While one of the aircraft hangers at R.A.F. Henlow provided an unusual venue for the Choir in the summer when they appeared at a fete arranged by the Biggleswade Round Table, the seaside concerts at Brighton, Eastbourne and Folkestone were still the main feature. Trips to the coast were just for the day with the Choir arriving about lunch time. After lunch the girls were free to enjoy themselves although the soloists would practise; then there would be a rehearsal for the full Choir after tea before the concert. The girls often arrived back in Luton at about 2.30am on Monday morning.

A concert at Worthing however caused quite a problem. The girls were to sing at the Pier Pavilion and although they experienced severe flooding on the joumey, made it safely to the coast. They managed to arrive in time to have lunch at the Town Hall with the Mayor and then give the concert. The weather did not improve and Peggy conferred with the local police while the girls were singing. She was advised not to attempt the journey home but what to do with the 62 girls and 45 parents?

During the interval an appeal was made for overnight accommodation and the good folk of Worthing were generous with their offers. Although it was already arranged there was a great deal of laughter when the first song of the second half was "All I Want is a Room Somewhere" from "My Fair Lady": much applause from the audience.

15 of the girls were accommodated in a convent, Mr and Mrs Davies and most of the parents were put up free in local hotels, just paying for their breakfast. Of course the girls had no night wear and Sandra was lent a nightdress with long ribbons down the front. She was grateful although she woke up in the night in a complete tangle.

The Choir started for home on Monday morning and with a lunch break in Windsor they arrived back in Luton in the late afternoon after making a 60 mile detour to avoid the floods. The girls had to miss school and work that day, a rare occurrence. For two girls it was their last concert and for three it was their first; it was certainly one to remember.

In October 1968 some of the girls sang at the Parents' Association Fair before the whole Choir went to sing at Wisbech. It was at this Fair that Mr Newham "slammed the Town" for not appreciating and supporting the Choir. As it was not appearing so much on radio and TV, it had lost its glamour appeal. New dresses were needed, new rehearsal rooms were required and vandals had smashed their pianos. The Fair did raise £250 and the Association was able to buy new stage shoes and replace the damaged pianos.

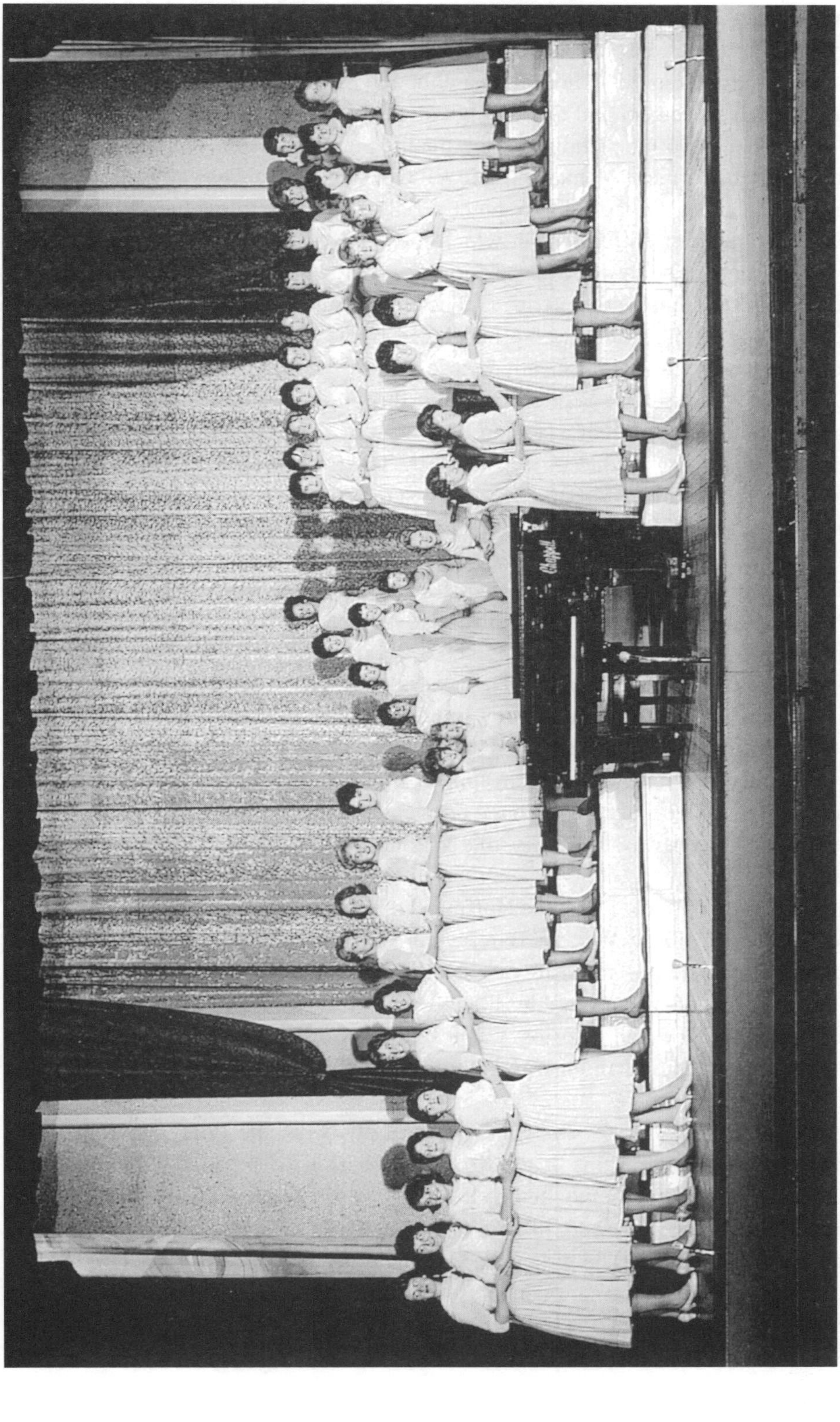

The Choir at Worthing. Photo Walter Gardiner (Worthing).

The outburst did provoke a response in the "Letters" column of the local paper, the writer citing the lure of TV as home entertainment, making people less keen to go out to concerts. Also the writer felt that although the Choir was local it still required adequate advertisement and this was not always forth-coming.

In January 1969 the Choir and the pianist Semprini were rivals to the Forsyte Saga, with the former two managing to fill Dunstable's Queensway Hall in spite of the popular appeal of the Sunday night serial. According to one newspaper report "As an example of the esteem in which the Choir is held in professional circles, Semprini not only agreed to perform in the same programme but also to accompany the Choir in two items, "Liebestraum" and Chaminade's "Automne". In the first half of the concert Semprini played a selection of classical music, in the second part were more light-hearted pieces.

The last weekend in September found the Choir in Clacton; on the Saturday singing in the Town Hall at a concert organised by Toc H and on the Sunday at the Princes Theatre in a concert organised by the Clacton and Vallence Twinning Association. The French group arrived late at the concert but the Choir were not put out and just accepted the change to the programme. The girls managed to sing "Les Allobroges", a song from the Vallence region, after just a couple of rehearsals and this was much appreciated by the French party who gave them a standing ovation.

The "Gala Rhapsody" at Watford in November had past and present members on the stage all the time. This meant the former members would not be buying tickets so, ever the business man, Mr Davies asked people to sell extra tickets to family and friends. The Luton and Fairey Bands appeared with the Choir and the guest conductor was the Choir's friend, Harry Mortimer.

In January 1970 the Choir again appeared with Semprini, this time at St. Albans. The concert was similar in style to the previous one at Dunstable. In February it was back to the Queensway Hall; this time William Davies (no relation) was the guest pianist.

The Choir, with the Ransome Hoffman and Pollard Works and Snibton Colliery and Thoreby Colliery Welfare Bands, were in a combined concert to start the Nottingham Music festival in July. When the girls arrived there was a mix up at the hotel and no food was available, though after a bit of a fuss some snacks were provided. The girls had also lost out in the food stakes at a previous concert in Croydon when the Salvation Army's Red Shield Band had eaten all the food while the girls were rehearsing.

The biggest events for the Choir in the '70's were the W.D. and H.O. Wills Brass Band Championships at the Royal Albert Hall where in 1972 the guest of honour was the Earl Mountbatten of Burma. The programme was in two parts, the competition being followed in the second half by a concert, which was also broadcast on the radio. The girls were singing as the "Rhapsody Chorus" - that was the present Choir and former members, with some of the latter, on a visit home from Canada and Australia, taking part.

Record sleeve from the W.D. and H.O .Wills Festival of Brass. Photo Bob Norman.

Luton Band entered one of the competions that year, under their Musical Director, Mr Albert Coupe, and won the National Challenge trophy, beating 19 other bands. Their prize was the Wills Silver Clef trophy and £100. The evening concert was conducted by Harry Mortimer and of course he was delighted with Luton's win. Ten coaches of Choir members and friends enjoyed the evening, a record was made and Sandra Goodman remembers it as a fantastic occasion, with a photograph of the "Rhapsody Chorus" and the Bands featured on the record sleeve.

The 1973 Championships were won by the Fairey Band and again the Choir and six bands, with Harry Mortimer, featured in the second half concert and broadcast. During the concert the organ went out of tune, the Choir ended up singing in a lower key and the "altos" were "singing in their boots". The audience joined the Choir and the bands in "Now thank we all our God".

Closer to home and again with the Luton Band was the first Arndale Concert for Christmas 1973. In aid of the Mayor, Bert King's Christmas appeal it was a sell out with an audience of 1000 people. S.G. Kitsell of Hastings St. installed the sound system in Smith's Square in the Arndale and described it as the most difficult local building they had dealt with for a concert. A sound expert spent three days testing the centre and the programme went off without a hitch.

There was a second Arndale concert the following year and although there were several bomb scares and it was felt to be rather risky having a large gathering of people in the Centre, the concert went ahead. Choir and Band members were issued with special passes to get into the Arndale for a rehearsal and the show was again successful.

It was Arthur and Gwen's Golden Wedding in September 1974 and there was a dinner and dance in their honour in the Ascot Room in Stockingstone Road. It was arranged as a surprise for Mr and Mrs Davies in appreciation of their lifetime devotion to the Luton Girls Choir and Mr Davies was presented with a record player from the Choir. A tribute to the couple by the Mayor, Councillor Hedley Lawrence, appeared in the local paper.

Mr Davies' birthday at Worthing. Photo Library Collection.

Christmas 1974 was the year when the girls also met Jimmy Saville, dining with him at Stoke Mandeville and watching Mr Davies enjoy one of Jimmy Saville's big cigars.

In the early '70s Mr Davies was beginning to find it hard work to carry on with the Choir. His health was beginning to fail and he also found it impossible to play the piano. He had little feeling in his fingers and could not feel the keys. For a few years Colin Smith, the well known local musician, played the piano at concerts, while Mr Davies concentrated on the conducting. Most pieces being sung were the "old faithfuls" regularly included in the concerts, as modern pieces would not have been right. Colin Smith had a sister in the Choir so he knew the repertoire and he just kept his eye on Mr Davies. At a "Gala Rhapsody", with the Band of the Royal Corps of Signals, it did happen that Mr Davies was conducting at one speed, the Band at another and the Choir at yet another.

There had been fewer concerts and there was a gradual winding down. The girls felt Mr Davies' sadness as he realised that the Choir's days were numbered and the last time the choir sang under their leader's direction was at the annual Christmas visit to Luton and Dunstable Hospital in 1975.

It was still a shock however when on January 30th 1976 a letter was sent to all Choir personnel which had many of them in tears.

Dear ...

This is to advise you formally that it is no longer possible for the Luton Girls Choir to continue to give concerts.

This arises sadly from the fact that Arthur Davies, the Choir's Founder and sole Musical Director, is advised by his doctor that the time has come for him to lay down his baton.

There has never been any question of the Choir operating under any other musical director, the Choir and Arthur Davies have always belonged together.

The nicest thing of course would be to have a splendid Farewell Concert but this would put a physical and emotional strain on Mr Davies which is not considered reasonable in the immediately foreseeable future.

Reluctantly therefore the Trustees have a duty, in conjunction with the Parents and Supporters Association, to take appropriate action consequent upon the cessation of the Choir activities, although it is proposed, for the time being at least, to maintain the Choir's legal existence and so safeguard the name of the Choir and Arthur's unique association with it.

There are some financial and other matters to resolve which may take a little while. ln due course you will be further advised. This letter is solely to tell you the present situation.

When hopefully at some later date, it is possible to arrange a suitable function at which the heartfelt thanks we all feel towards Arthur and Gwen Davies can be expressed, the opportunity will be taken without delay.

Yours Sincerely Richard Hopkins. Chairman of Trustees of Luton Girls Choir.

When the news broke that the Luton Girls Choir was at its end, the sad news appeared in many of the national daily papers. In February 1976 at the age of 78 Mr Davies gave an interview to Peter Ruff from Radio 4 for the BBC. Mr Davies said the girls had altered over the years and latterly needed to be treated differently. They were better educated and expected more and he had to be a stern disciplinarian. The girls still knew the standard he expected. He also said he thought the Choir had really taken off after the Richard Tauber Memorial Concert in the Albert Hall.

At least one official body, the Luton Ratepayers Association, felt it was time the town honoured one of their remarkable "sons" and called for two tributes; a concert with Mr Davies as the special guest and for him to be made a Freeman of the Borough. Colin Smith was also lobbying for Mr Davies to receive this honour and on October 5th 1976 Luton Council actually decided to publicly acknowledge Mr Davies' contribution to the town. The girls were sent an official letter from the Chief Executive inviting them to the special ceremony which was held in the Council Chamber. Mr Davies was taken there from Hitchin hospital where he was recovering from a fall. He had been taken ill at a New Year's party and subsequently suffered a slight stroke. Members of the Choir sat in the gallery and heard Councillor Vivian Dunnington propose the resolution conferring the honour. He described Mr Davies as the heart, soul, brain and power of the Choir which was an enormous success story of international fame.

The Council also commissioned a bust, entitled "The Singing Girl", from Harpenden sculptress Miss Dora Barrett. The girl was modelled on Janet Bandy, a member of the Choir. Janet had appeared on the cover of one of the souvenir brochures and this was used as a basis. The bust was mounted on a plinth in Luton Central Library and unveiled the evening before Mr Davies received his "Freedom".

In November 1976 Mr Davies was again brought to Luton by ambulance, this time to St. Mary's Church hall to meet the last members of the Choir. The girls received an Illuminated Address of appreciation from him, 14 of them receiving clocks for long service. Miss Lynda Janes had been with the Choir for more than 11 years and was the longest serving member at its disbandment.

"The Singing Girl". Photo Bob Norman.

Mr Davies and his wife were in "Elmtrees" in December and this time it was their turn to listen to the Choir sing at Christmas.

Early in 1977 Mr Davies was very ill and asked the Trustees to do what they could to protect the name of the Luton Girls Choir, so that his unique connection with it would not be broken now he could no longer direct it. The Choir was something he had nurtured and he felt it would not be the same with anybody else in charge. Girls came and went but the sound was always the same. He also felt another director might be tempted to exploit the Choir for financial gain.

The Trustees felt that the best way to do this was to remain in being as long as it was necessary. Neither the girls nor the Parents and Supporters Association wanted to continue under another director. The Trust technically had the legal power of authority to appoint the Musical Director so they just did not appoint anybody. Richard Hopkins, Chairman of the Trust, wound up the affairs and the money left was transferred to the Arthur Davies Memorial Fund.

On May 31st 1977 a truly remarkable man died.

On June 8th a funeral service was held at St Mary's Church before Mr Davies was cremated at the Vale. The Town dignitaries were there for a final farewell, the Mayor Cllr Ken Furlong, the Ex Mayor Cllr Frank Lester and members of Luton Council. The service was conducted by both the Vicar of Luton, Rev. Christopher Mayhew and the Luton Methodist Minister, Rev. Maldwyn Williams. A special tribute was paid to Mr Davies by his boyhood friend, Sir Harry Mortimer, who said from the pulpit that he felt very cross that the Town Council had only seen fit to make Mr Davies a Freeman of the Borough a few months before he died.

Mr Gore who, as well as being a trustee, was secretary of the Luton and Dunstable Chamber of Commerce and Industry, said :- "I run missions all over the world, yet out there instead of people associating Luton with hats and Vauxhall Motors, people always refer to the Choir and Mr Davies. Mr Davies was a man who has not been fully recognised in Luton and it is a great pity nothing is being carried on. He is not recognised in Luton as the great man he is". Mr Hopkins said the feeling was widespread that it was Mr Davies' distinct musical gift and ability to inspire young people that made the Choir and that it would not be the same without him.

Mr Davies had previously requested that no flowers be sent but donations made to the National Children's Home. There was however a wreath of white flowers surrounding a blue treble clef, from the Choir. The Choir sang "Panis Angelicus" and the "Easter Hymn". Peggy Coggins said that the Choir had sung as well if not better than she had ever heard them; Mr Davies would have been proud of them.

The Ratepayers' other idea, of a concert, took place on November 5th 1977. There was no guest of honour, the concert was a memorial tribute entitled "Music you Know and Love." The Parish Church was packed to capacity with seats even in the aisles. 700 tickets had been sold without the concert being advertised, so 500 people were given a chance to hear the Choir at the final rehearsal.

Former Choir members were in the audience including some from Australia and New Zealand. The evening was introduced by Marie Birchenough and Colin Smith played the piano. During the evening Mr Richard Hopkins, Chairman of the Luton Girls Choir Trust, thanked the girls on behalf of the Borough for all their hard work over the many years of the Choir's existence.

93 girls sang all the old favourites including "The Emperor Waltz", "Tales from the Vienna Woods" and "Down in the Forest", the first half closing with "The Lost

Memorial Concert in St. Mary's Church, Luton, 1977. Photo Luton News.

Chord". The second half included one of Mr Davies's favourite items "Still as the Night" the solo being sung by Lynda Janes. There was also a selection from "Carousel". Of course the Richard Tauber connection was mentioned and the Choir sang "You are my Heart's Delight" and "My Heart and I". The concert ended with the "Easter Hymn", June Gascoigne singing the solo. During this number the audience stood in homage to Mr Arthur Davies M.B.E.

Two years later, on June 6th 1979, a bronze bust of Mr Davies was unveiled in Luton Music Library by his old friend Sir Harry Mortimer. It had been bought with the money raised by the two tribute concerts, as the girls thought it would be a suitable memorial. It was sculpted by Dora Barrett, the same sculptress who had produced the "Singing Girl" and she together with the Mayor Cllr. Bill Copeland and his wife and sixty former members of the Choir attended the unveiling. After the ceremony the guests watched a film of one of the Choir's greatest triumphs, the Australasia Tour.

Harry Mortimer unveiling the bust of Arthur Davies. Photo Sandra Aldridge.

The Luton Girls Choir was definitely a product of its age and could not have flourished today as it did then. It came into being before the days of mass, sophisticated forms of entertainment, during an age more innocent than the 1990's. In the 1970's it was facing stiff competition on the music front as well as the difficulty of commitment from the girls to the choir itself. Pop music was all the rage and girls matured more quickly, getting married earlier or pursuing further education at colleges and universities away from Luton. There were some who thought the Choir should have continued after Mr Davies's death. It was better that it ceased while it was still well loved, taking with it the sound which Arthur Davies made his own.

Bust of Arthur Davies. Photo Bob Norman.

Lynda Janes and Alison Nicol at the unveiling of the bust of Arthur Davies. Photo Sandra Aldridge.

Chapter Fifteen

After the Choir

Reunions

In 1986 it was 50 years since the formation of the Luton Girls Choir and the idea of a grand reunion was mooted. Jill Gibson wrote to ITV's "Breakfast TV" and she, Peggy Coggins and Madge Moran, née Pakes, one of the original choir members, appeared on the show, being interviewed about the Choir and making an appeal for ex-members to contact ITV. There was a huge response and 250 former members of the Choir eventually gathered for a Reunion and Tribute to Mr Davies.

Nicholas Phillips allowed them to use Luton Hoo as a venue and many local concerns helped in other ways. Whitbreads gave the wine for the evening and Haydens also helped with the drinks. Icknield School lent rostra for the girls to stand on while singing and Vauxhall and BBC Radio Bedfordshire helped with the production of a souvenir brochure. The BBC also subsidised the meal.

Malcolm Singer produced a series of half hour programmes broadcast locally on a Sunday afternoon, entitled "Girls in Blue". Six sessions told the story of the Choir, with personal recollections from former members and people who had known Mr Davies. The members said :

"Mr Davies knew what sound he wanted and the girls responded. The sound is recognised even today, so strong was the teaching, not just singing but feeling. He directed them to sing from the heart.

He was a powerful man, shrewd and would nearly always get his own way. If he didn't, everyone knew about it. The mould of men who dedicated their life to music was broken when he died.

He was a man who could inspire the girls and bring out things they did not know they possessed. He formed their characters teaching them self control, tolerance and patience.

There was a magic with the Choir that you did not get elsewhere.

One of the younger members thought it was a treat to wear a little make up on the stage. She did not wear it normally.

The Choir's seaside visits went on long after other people doing the same thing ceased. Entertainment Officers had a soft spot for the Choir and a long memory. The Choir could still fill the halls and they were getting bookings right up to the end. Roy Darby said "He had the courage to stick with what he created; the Choir was unique when it began and they sang what people wanted to hear".

Sir Harry Mortimer said, "He rehearsed the girls till they were perfect, even if they were not particularly musical".

At the Reunion. Photo Three Counties Radio.

Richard Hopkins thought Mr and Mrs Davies were the right people in the right place at the right time. Gwen had the knack of keeping Arthur on a rein; she was motherly and he was a showman and enjoyed riding on a wave of publicity.

The Millennium Reunion

The year 2000, recognised by the world as an important date, was also special to former Choir members for another reason; it was Peggy Coggins' eightieth birthday and the two events presented a good excuse for a Millennium Reunion. In October 160 former Choir Girls met again, in the Riverside Suite at the Vauxhall Recreation Centre, to sing the songs they loved and reminisce about the good times which they had enjoyed. In many instances mother and daughter celebrated together. As well as members from all over Britain there were people from America, Canada and Australia who had arranged a visit home to coincide with the reunion.

Jill Gibson had worked hard behind the scenes and each guest was presented with a souvenir brochure as a memento of the evening. It contained a collection of Choir photographs, the words of some of their favourite songs and a list of all the people attending. On display were more photos from the Choir archives and these, together with the girls' personal photos, provided material for much talk and laughter. A splendid way to celebrate the year 2000.

The legacy of the Choir

The Choir was a way of life to all of those who sang in it over the years. They considered it a great honour to be chosen and enjoyed the good things it brought them, such as the chance to mix with the famous and to travel, especially in the early days when most girls of their age did not have that opportunity. The girls gained a good grounding for life; it gave them confidence and a belief in themselves but also a sense of humility. They learnt the ability to mix with all walks of life; one weekend they could be staying with a wealthy host in a big house, the next in a terrace. One concert would be with well known stars in a spacious and prestigious venue, the next time they could be singing in a hospital or church hall. Every member I interviewed thought it was worth the cost of giving up the precious week ends and withstanding the teasing of her friends.

Comments from some of the parents showed that they too appreciated what it did for their daughters. One father's words re his daughter's trip to Australasia. "She went away a young girl, she came back a young lady".

Even right at the end this feeling was very strong and the words of Sheila Goodman, wife of the last Chairman of the Parents and Supporters Association, sums up what the Choir meant to all who belonged in one way or another. "Having two daughters in the Choir gave us a family closeness which kept us together for a number of years at a time when teenagers of the same age were "doing their own thing". It was at a time when society was changing and leisure time meant much more than in the previous decades, so life took on a new kind of dedication.

Hairstyles were changing, fashions were often a little eccentric but none of this took over from the dedication and loyalty still given to Mr Davies. The girls received excellent training from Arthur Davies and most of them have kept music in their lives as a hobby and one sees their talents regularly shining through at concerts and musicals that are held in the area.

Staying with complete strangers and conversing at all levels has been part of their education and helped to give individuals confidence, besides learning quite a lot about England, charities and the like through their travels.

All conscientious parents look to their children's general behaviour and acceptance of discipline. In this, the respect that the choirgirls held for Mr Davies was such that the discipline he demanded was accepted without question. The girls' upbringing was enhanced by the pleasure the Choir gave to audiences both large and small and they gained confidence by meeting so many people in all walks of life".

In the words of the man himself. "It was an Organisation of Good Intent".

Chapter Sixteen

Mr Davies and Peggy Coggins

Arthur Davies M.B.E. Photo S. Theodorson, Luton

In 1897 Mr Davies was born into a family interested in both music and the Methodist Church, his parents being actively involved with the Church at Round Green. Mr Davies senior was Superintendent of the Sunday School on the corner of Ramridge and Hitchin roads and secretary to the Trustees of the later building in Hitchin Road. His mother was involved with the Women's Bright Hour and was secretary to the Tract Society. His father also had a choir in the Church at Round Green and later, at 14 years old, the younger Davies played the piano for the soloist at the Harvest Festival in the New Wesleyan Chapel.

At the tender age of five years old the young boy was having his first piano lessons and when he was seven he asked his father to change his music teacher because she seemed more interested in the social side than in his music. His new teacher was a strict disciplinarian who made him work hard.

Arthur actually sang his first solo at 8 years old in Gravenhurst Methodist Church and together with school friend Harry Mortimer, at the age of 9 or 10 years old, was performing in local charity concerts. He played the piano and sang while Harry Mortimer played the cornet. They also appeared at the Old Palace Theatre, Mill Street and their signature tune was "Happy Moments Day by Day." The fees earned in this way went to pay for more lessons.

Harry Mortimer's father, Fred, was conductor of the Luton Band and his son later followed in his footsteps, becoming a famous professional musician. Harry Mortimer described Arthur as "an enthusiastic amateur whose work for music was a labour of love".

At 17 years old Arthur Davies already had strong views on choral singing, stating that choral music had been grossly neglected in England and he intended to do something about it. He had an urge to revolutionise it and make the choir as appealing to the eye as to the ear. When he was 18 years old he had his own group of eight people at Round Green Church, called the Cremona Concert party.

His musical education already included a study of both the piano and organ when his father taught him the rudiments of skilled and sensitive conducting. Later he took courses under Mr John Fry, a famous tutor at the Trinity College of Music and occasionally Arthur would conduct or accompany his father's choir. He also had singing lessons from Dawson Greer.

When Arthur left school he started work at George Kents but his prime interest and hobby was music. He thought he would lose contact with the musical world when he volunteered for the forces during the First World War. Instead he was asked to organise Sunday concerts at Woolwich Town Hall and this provided him with the good experience of engaging artistes of international repute and of accompanying them during rehearsals which would prove invaluable later on.

He was connected with the Luton Choral Society for 29 years, becoming the deputy conductor in 1931 and the actual Choral Society conductor in 1940. However, it had been when at 24 years old he became Choirmaster of Wellington Street Baptist Church Choir, the largest church choir in Luton, that he was able to really start putting his ideas into practice. He believed that good voices were the gift of God and should be encouraged and developed so that the owner of the voice could give pleasure to others and herself by using it to its best advantage.

Mr Davies was married to Gwen in 1924 and although they did not have children of their own they were surrounded by girls for forty years. In 1940 they were able to provide a home for one little girl who was evacuated from London and, although it did not happen quite as Eamon Andrews said it did, Anne Henry lived with them for several years. She could not be left at home when the Choir was at a concert so she was allowed to join; fortunately she had a reasonably good voice. Her real father died at the end of the war, so it was Mr and Mrs Davies who arranged the wedding at St Christopher's Church in Round Green and Mr Davies who escorted her up the aisle to marry Peter Evans, the brother of one of the Choir girls.

Anne comments on her life at that time: "It must have been difficult for a childless couple to take a total stranger into their home, but somehow we bonded so quickly and over the months and years I really did feel like their very own child and was treated as their own child. They guided me, cared for me and taught me so much and their influence on me has lasted all my life".

Arthur Davies took part in most of Luton's musical activities and during the Second World War he was involved in the "Holidays at Home" programmes with concerts in Wardown Park and in the local cinemas.

In 1946 the Choir was becoming well known and Mr Davies was appointed as a member of the Council of the National Federation of Musical Societies. He was also at that time supporting the National Children's Homes with the Choir Tours and he became a Life Governor of the Homes in 1947.

Mr Davies's actual business was as an agricultural agent for Soil Fertility Dunn's Ltd; he did not make any money from his Choir activities. The contacts made were helpful in his work but his job did perhaps suffer slightly as he did not make as many personal visits as he should have done.

His intention was to train and conduct a choir of young voices and to interest youngsters in good music, including well written light music as well as the classics. He could not bear to think that other people were likely to miss one of the greatest joys of this life through lack of opportunity or training. One quote described his zeal in the matter of getting folk to appreciate good music as comparable to that of the early Evangelists in their self appointed task of spreading the Gospel.

In 1953 there were 26 girls choirs in the country and Mr Davies would encourage them wherever he could, regarding new groups as a sign of the Luton Girls Choir's success in arousing interest in music among young people.

He said running the Choir was 40% psychology and 60% music and he used the psychological approach when auditioning the girls. In times of pressure he would appeal to the girls themselves, often via a letter, stating what was needed and implying that he felt the girl would respond in a positive manner. Of course she did. He was a great believer in letters and would write to the girls before any big event or tour, explaining what was happening and what he expected the girls to do. There was a three page one for the Australasian trip.

He believed in happiness; to sing, a girl must be happy and if she was happy she would sing. He taught the girls to put all they could into life and they would find they got 100% dividends.

His standards of behaviour were high. e.g. "Ambassadors of the Town" and he was a very moral man. Often during rehearsals he would stop and explain the meaning behind the words and give the girls a little talk on aspects of life. Many of the girls remember his words today. Anne's comments again: "Mr Davies disciplined us all in his gentle way, we did not waste our rehearsal hours, his patience in teaching us was infinite and I am sure that each one of us has in some way been wonderfully blessed to have been members of his Choir. Our problems were his problems and he quietly helped many girls to overcome difficulties during the years. Mrs Davies was an unassuming, unselfish and very supportive wife and their love for each other was never dimmed".

(This sentiment was echoed by the many former Choir girls who have been good enough to help with this book. I literally felt that each one would have done anything for him, held him in high esteem and felt he had a profound influence on their life.)

He always observed the 2 minutes silence on November 11th. If the Choir was on tour he would stop the coach and if they were in rehearsal he would say it was time and the girls would be quiet. There was no giggling or nudging, just a natural dignity.

His performance presentation was respected by all the professionals. One writer described it thus :- "The most important contributing factor to the Choir's success is undoubtedly Mr Arthur Davies's careful organisation and training and the bond of understanding between him and the Choir. Every detail for the welfare of the girls, for their appearance and their deportment on stage is carefully worked out. Their poise and self possession proves that an amateur organisation need never be amateurish." Perhaps the best summing up of this unusual man was by the Rev. A.J. Bayliss in the St Mary's Methodist Circuit Magazine in 1951, when the Choir visited Cornwall. "There is the genius, leadership and genial personality of Arthur Davies. In him, coupled with great musical ability, are just those properties of leadership which alone could lead a choir through the years, to the place that this one now occupies in the affections of millions of people. He has the capacity to "think big" and to take risks. For the Choir he has made great sacrifices of both time and money. In their interests and the presentation through them of great music, his life has for many years been one long "extra mile". It is upon this foundation stone that this wonderful Choir has been built up".

Peggy Coggins

Peggy was born in Luton in 1920 and was a pupil at Christ Church School until she was 12 years old. That year her father died and as her mother could not afford to send her to the Luton High School she attended Chapel Street Senior Girls. Her parents were not particularly musical but she can remember her mother was always singing. This could have been responsible for Peggy's love of music from an early age, first the enjoyment of being taken to the Sunday School Anniversaries at Chapel Street Methodist Church and later singing in them herself.

She envied her friends who were members of the Luton Girls Choir but at that time her loyalty was to her own church choir and she did not have time for both. At 20 she did become a member of the Luton Choral Society and later held the post of secretary, a post which carried an honorarium of twenty guineas a year.

During the war the Choral Society took part in broadcasts for the BBC which was based in Bedford and Peggy, like members of the Luton Girls Choir, sang with the "names" of the day. The Choral Society recorded a special programme to be broadcast when the war was over.

Prior to her father's death, plans were already afoot for the family to move to Welwyn Garden City on his appointrnent as resident electrician for an engineering firm but in view of the changed circumstances Peggy remained in Luton with her mother and brother. When she left school at fourteen she went to work in the office of Currant and Creak, the hat manufacturers.

The hours were long and she often did not finish until 7.30 in the evening so about nine months later she joined her cousin at the Skefko Ball Bearing Company as an office junior. Peggy went to evening classes to learn shorthand and typing and this led to several internal promotions. During the war she was lucky enough to be in a reserved occupation as secretary to one of the Swedish bosses of the firm. She was there for 14 years.

It was an advertisement in the local paper which brought about the dramatic change. Mr Davies wanted a secretary and Peggy telephoned him to enquire about the job. She knew him casually from the Choral Society and obviously by repute as conductor of the Luton Girls Choir. It so happened that the vacancy had already been filled but twelve months later Mr Davies sent her a letter to say his secretary was leaving and was Peggy still interested in the position? This was in 1949 and Peggy was with him for 28 years. It became more a way of life than just a job.

Peggy Coggins and members of the Choir. Photo Sheila Pilkington.

Her office duties were very mixed, varying from business routine in connection with Mr Davies' agricultural agency to matters appertaining to the Choir. She eventually spent about 70% of her time on the latter, even though Patricia Corley was engaged as a shorthand typist primarily to deal with correspondence.

Outside of office hours Peggy's special responsibility was the management of the girls. This Herculean task included going everywhere with the Choir, checking that everyone was on the coach and arranging the accommodation on the tours. It was her job to allocate the girls to an appropriate family, a choice they would try to influence if they liked the look of a particular escort at the end of a concert. There was also the organisation of the girls going on to the stage and using the dressing room, especially in small halls where space could be very limited.

She enjoyed looking after the girls although sometimes she felt she was a bit hard on them; she knew she had to be firm but she often became their confidante, helping with boyfriend troubles and the like.

Peggy left the Choral Society at the same time as Mr Davies in 1960 but she remained a member of the Luton Amateur Operatic and Dramatic Society to which she has now given over fifty years of service both on stage and in an administrative capacity. She has been the secretary for 36 years. She played mostly comedy roles, her favourite character part being Yenta the matchmaker in "Fiddler on the Roof".

The VicWardians started in 1956 and Peggy was a member from the beginning until it disbanded 35 years later. A small group of people provided "old time" style entertainment and she took part in most of the 860 shows which were staged, mainly for charity.

After the death of Mr Davies when the office was finally closed, Peggy worked for about eight years in the Electoral Registration Department of the Town Hall. She then helped out at intervals before starting to travel annually to Australia. Her first visit was in 1988 and now she spends the English winter months with her schoolfriend in Perth. In 1997 she was interviewed about the Luton Girls Choir by Mr W.J. Ferrell for The Oral History Association of Western Australia.

Appendices

Poem to commemorate the Australasia Tour in 1959

We have just been to London to see our girls go,
In two shades of blue they really made a grand show.
Hats, gloves, shoes and handbags in white,
To everyone there they made a grand sight.

They went to the airport in red and green buses,
Those girls dressed in blue, great Luton lasses,
There was Vera and Gayda and Carol and Joan,
There were twins June and Mary, hardly alone,
There was Barbara and Jennifer, Patricia and Beryl,
There was Julie and Jane, Wendy and Meryl.

Too many to name, but they should all be mentioned,
But I can't manage that, with the best of intention.
Amongst all those girls went a man and two ladies,
Peggy Coggins secretary and Mr and Mrs Arthur Davies.

We were proud of them then and shall be again,
They will be stopping at Rome, Beruit and Barhrein,
Karachi, Calcutta and to Bangkok,
On Wednesday night that's their first stop.
On Thursday at 6 again on their way,
Arrive at Manilla just after midday,
Then on to Biak where they are due to arrive,
According to schedule at 9.45.

Some 24 hours in the plane once again,
Then stop once more before they get to Brisbane.
That's at 2.50am when they are due in
At the Northern Australian town of Darwin.

They are due for a rest for just a few days,
This is thought best to get used to new ways.
New things they'll see, new things they'll eat,
And just to lie back and put up their feet.

This year they'll enjoy an Australian spring
And then like the birds they'll be starting to sing,
At Brisbane, Toowomba and Brisbane again,
Ipswich and Southport, no your not seeing things,
Then back once again to the Festival Hall.
Not London my dears, it's Brisbane's last call,
They go to the town of Wollongong,

To Newcastle Stadium, not where Geordies come from.
No need to worry they'll be setting the pace,
Seven days in Sydney, a "Capitol" place.
Katomba and Batherest and Lithgo and all
And then on to Orange where next day they'll call.

Then once again over the seas they shall roam,
When they will be farthest from Luton and home.
They are due in New Zealand at the end of September,
That will surely for them be a date to remember.

They will go to Dunedin at the Town Hall to sing,
The best of their talents New Zealand to bring.
Invercargill, Timaru and Christchurch St James,
Each city they go to the pattern's the same.

To Wellington, Palmerston, Hamilton too,
To Auckland Town Hall for five days or so,
Then Ballarat in Australia where I am told
Some years ago they were digging for gold.
A school matinee here at half past ten,
They repeat this performance at Melbourne again.

Before they go on to Gambis mountain and all
And on once again to Adelaide Town Hall,
There is a PSA concert for the Rev. White,
Then they leave for Adelaide that very same night.

For nights in the Odeon, Adelaide town,
To their very last call of all they move on.
From the seventh of November His Majesty's, Perth,
They sing here again for all they are worth.

Before they embark once more in their plane
to come back to Luton, their home town again,
They will bring to the town laurels anew,
They will come back again to me and to you.

Let us be thankful for those girls dressed in blue,
They give to the world a jolly good do.
Let the town be happy and be mighty proud
For the girls dressed in blue, Arthur Davies's crowd.

There is more than a little poetic licence in this poem.

Their Finest Hour
One of the poems composed and read by Zena Rocliffe

London, eleven o'clock by Big Ben's chime,
September the third, nineteen thirty nine:
From end to end of England, ran
The words of Chamberlain to every man.
"WAR" the word in every mouth
From east to west, north to south.
The peace we tried so hard to gain,
The peace we sought - in vain
Was driven fast from every head,
And war reigned there instead.
Now, "ON GUARD" England stands,
With her comrades of other lands.
Big Ben stands a symbol now:
A tall and regal sentinel,
Symbolic of all that's true and great
In this world of War and hate.
The old church bells ring out no more
As, happily in days of yore,
They summoned folk to come and pray;
If now they ring the bells will say
Stand by! Invasion's on the way.
When fires rage in many a town,
When deadly bombs come streaming down,
When death rains from above,
To claim the friends and homes we love,
The Bulldog Spirit stands the test
And Britishers give of their best.
"GO TO IT" rings the hearty cry,
Go to it lads, and do, or die.
So steadily we carry on
And work with smile and song;
Do any dare to question why
Men give their all, and die,
And suffer for Freedom's sake,
As men of old at burning stake.
On the cross of Calvary
Our Christ hung in agony;

He suffered to cleanse the earth:
Now is the chance to show our worth,
Now the works of destiny
Have given us our Calvary.
And by fair word and noble deed
May we follow the Almighty's lead.
And with His help may we oppress
The forces of evil and wickedness.

Travelling song of the Choir
To the tune of "She wears red feathers."

We wear blue dresses with little red velvet bows,
We wear blue dresses with little red velvet bows,
We live on psychology and "Lift up your hearts"
And when we have a song to sing we sing it in three parts.

We are the Luton Girls Choir, we practice every Friday
Old Arthur E comes round to see if our red shoes are ti- i- dy.
He says "We'll sing the Snow" and all the girls say "Oh"
We'd rather sing like dear old Bing, but Arthur E says "No".

We sing for the Children's Home, to make the children happy.
We'd like to see our Arthur E pin on a baby's nappy.
We heard a robin sing and whistle in Pedro
So can we sing like Nat the King but Arthur still says "No".

"Someday"

Someday we shall meet again
I'll find you whereever you are.
Dreams we'll mend at the journey's end
And our hearts will follow their star.

Someday though the world is dark
The sunshine will smile through the rain,
Love will last till the storm is past
And we meet again - meet again.

Subscribers

To 30th April 2001

Sandra Aldridge (nee Goodman)
Diana Allen (nee Evans)
Anne Allsopp
Edena Ashton
Patricia Aspell (nee Amos)
Jean Baldwin (nee Barden)
Lesley Catherine Barker (nee Henry)
Julie Newsom (nee Barrett)
Pamela Barrett (nee Minchall)
Lorna Baxter (nee Porter)
Marie Birchenough (nee Robinson)
Elsie M. Brelsford (nee Heley)
Joan Brewer (nee Folks)
Yvonne Buckingham (nee James)
Barbara Cain (nee Norris)
Marion Cain (nee Webb)
Moira E. Cann (nee Williams)
Jose Canning (nee Abbiss)
June Carnegie (nee Ekins)
Dilys Clark (nee Jones)
Jill Clements (nee Shawcross)
Teresa Crocker (nee Burnham)
Elsie Cropper (nee Routledge)
Tina Cross (nee Jeffs)
Jill Curtis (nee Banks)
Sheila Davies (nee Land)
Edna Dayton (nee Broughall)
Freda Dix (nee Smith)
Jose Dobing
Josephine Driscoll (nee Fisher)
June Driver (nee Parcell)
James Dyer
Trina Earnshaw (nee Jones)
Anne Evans (nee Henry)
Carole Evason (nee Thirkettle)
June Finch (nee Burgess)
Bridget Foster (nee Ruskin)
Sheila Franklin (nee Brockway)
Hazel Freisenbruch (nee Martin)
Pat Gale (nee Esling)
Maisie Garner (nee Wheeler)
Doreen M.Gayton (nee Cain)
Jill Gibson (nee Taylor)
Sheila & George Goodman
Eddie & Rosemary Grabham
Shirley Grant (nee Barker)
Jacqueline Greening (nee Dale)
Mrs G.Haines
Judith Hammond (nee Summerfield)
Gilda Harris (nee Doyle)
Diana Hawkins (daughter of Mr A.R.Hills - choir treasurer)
Margaret Hawkins (nee Jones)
Sheila Hawtin (nee Baynham)
Mary Hill (nee Ekins)
Mrs A.R. Hills
Zena D. Horne (nee Scowen)
Marjorie Horrell (nee Wood)
Miss C.J. Howe
Jacqueline Howe (nee Goodman)
Gayda Hughes (nee Davison)
Paul Hunt
Pauline Huska (nee Grigg)
Sherrie-Jane Jackson (nee Clements)
Judith Jervis (nee Twigg)
Roy W. Joyner
June Kilby (nee Kinnear)
Coral King (nee Anthony)
Adrienne Lane (nee Cooper)
Shirley Latter (nee Whatley)
Mr. D.W. Lewis B.A. (Hons)
June Lusted (nee Wheeler)
Betty Manton (nee Bird)
Carolyn McConnell (nee Jessop)
Marilyn McHale (nee Owen)
Barbara Meazey (d/d) (nee Hare)
Stella Molton (nee Parrott)
Marie Morris (nee Fisher)
Alison Nicol
Shirley Noller
Anne N. Norcross
Paddy & Bob Norman
Marion L.Oades (nee Large)
Vera O'Dell (nee Chance)
Claire Olney (nee Williams)
April Orsag (nee Kemp)
Olive Owen (nee Garner)
Barbara Page (nee Oakley)
Doreen Parrott (nee Rawlings)
Pat Parrott (nee Willis)
Margaret Patten (nee Hale)
Janet Phillips-Lewis (nee Addie)
Nancy Platt (nee Burr)
Wendy Pollard (nee Sutton)
Iris Porter (nee Price)
Jean Preece
Iris Purves (nee Sear)
Angela Reed (nee Chapman)
Jennifer Reed
Beryl Rogers (nee Anstee)
Mary Rogers (nee Willett)
Monica Ryan (nee Cross)
Jennifer Savage (nee Dodd)
Gillian Sharp (nee Wicks)
Linda Shearn (nee Raven)
Mr. S.G. Sheppard
Susan E.A. Slough (nee Bishop)
Gillian Smith (nee Clark)
Mary Smith
Thelma Smith (nee Rootham)
Valerie Stephenson (nee Snead)
Daphne Stillwell (nee Waller)
Brenda Stone (nee Bainbridge)
Beryl Symonds (nee Brown)
Mary Tate (nee Armstrong)
Gillian Tennant (nee Smith)
Lynda Todd (nee Harry)
Dianne Tompkins (nee Mercer)
Anne Townrow (nee Felmingham)
Carole Vanschagen (nee Gibbons)
Valerie Venables (nee Toynton)
Irene Wagstaff (nee Jones)
Jill Waller
Dianne Walters (nee Philpott)
Christine Ward (nee Harris)
Christine Watson (nee Cawson)
Rita Webb (nee Sharpe)
Stuart Wigg
Deborah Wilkinson (nee Gibson)
Elizabeth Wilson (nee Stanbrook-Evans)
Jean Wilson (nee Fountain)
Margaret Wood (nee Matthews)

Books Published by THE BOOK CASTLE

CHANGES IN OUR LANDSCAPE: Aspects of Bedfordshire, Buckinghamshire and the Chilterns 1947-1992: Eric Meadows. Over 350 photographs from the author's collection spanning nearly 50 years.

COUNTRYSIDE CYCLING IN BEDFORDSHIRE, BUCKINGHAMSHIRE AND HERTFORDSHIRE: Mick Payne. Twenty rides on and off-road for all the family.

PUB WALKS FROM COUNTRY STATIONS: Bedfordshire and Hertfordshire: Clive Higgs. Fourteen circular country rambles, each starting and finishing at a railway station and incorporating a pub stop at a mid way point.

PUB WALKS FROM COUNTRY STATIONS: Buckinghamshire and Oxfordshire: Clive Higgs. Circular rambles incorporating pub-stops.

LOCAL WALKS: South Bedfordshire and North Chilterns: Vaughan Basham. Twenty-seven thematic circular walks.

LOCAL WALKS: North and Mid Bedfordshire: Vaughan Basham. Twenty-five thematic circular walks.

FAMILY WALKS: Chilterns South: Nick Moon. Thirty 3 to 5 mile circular walks.

FAMILY WALKS: Chilterns North: Nick Moon. Thirty shorter circular walks.

CHILTERN WALKS: Hertfordshire, Bedfordshire and North Bucks: Nick Moon.

CHILTERN WALKS: Buckinghamshire: Nick Moon.

CHILTERN WALKS: Oxfordshire and West Buckinghamshire: Nick Moon. A trilogy of circular walks, in association with the Chiltern Society. Each volume contains 30 circular walks.

OXFORDSHIRE WALKS: Oxford, the Cotswolds and the Cherwell Valley: Nick Moon.

OXFORDSHIRE WALKS: Oxford, the Downs and the Thames Valley: Nick Moon. Two volumes that complement Chiltern Walks: Oxfordshire, and complete coverage of the county, in association with the Oxford Fieldpaths Society. Thirty circular walks in each.

THE D'ARCY DALTON WAY: Nick Moon. Long-distance footpath across the Oxfordshire Cotswolds and Thames Valley, with various circular walk suggestions.

THE CHILTERN WAY: Nick Moon. A guide to the new 133 mile circular Long-Distance Path through Bedfordshire, Buckinghamshire,Hertfordshire and Oxfordshire, as planned by the Chiltern Society.

JOURNEYS INTO BEDFORDSHIRE: Anthony Mackay. Foreword by The Marquess of Tavistock, Woburn Abbey. A lavish book of over 150 evocative ink drawings.

COCKNEY KID & COUNTRYMEN: Ted Enever. The Second World War remembered by the children of Woburn Sands and Aspley Guise. A six year old boy is evacuated from London's East End to start life in a Buckinghamshire village.

BUCKINGHAM AT WAR: Pip Brimson. Stories of courage, humour and pathos as Buckingham people adapt to war.
WINGS OVER WING: The Story of a World War II Bomber Training Unit: Mike Warth. The activities of RAF Wing in Buckinghamshire.
JOURNEYS INTO BUCKINGHAMSHIRE: Anthony Mackay. Superb line drawings plus background text: large format landscape gift book.
BUCKINGHAMSHIRE MURDERS: Len Woodley. Nearly two centuries of nasty crimes.
WINGRAVE: A Rothschild Village in the Vale: Margaret and Ken Morley. Thoroughly researched and copiously illustrated survey of the last 200 years in this lovely village between Aylesbury and Leighton Buzzard.
HISTORIC FIGURES IN THE BUCKINGHAMSHIRE LANDSCAPE: John Houghton. Major personalities and events that have shaped the county's past, including Bletchley Park.
TWICE UPON A TIME: John Houghton. North Bucks short stories loosely based on fact.
SANCTITY AND SCANDAL IN BEDS AND BUCKS: John Houghton. A miscellany of unholy people and events.
MANORS and MAYHEM, PAUPERS and PARSONS: Tales from Four Shires: Beds., Bucks., Herts. and Northants: John Houghton. Little known historical snippets and stories.
THE LAST PATROL: Policemen killed on duty while serving the Thames Valley: Len Woodley.
FOLK: Characters and Events in the History of Bedfordshire and Northamptonshire: Vivienne Evans. Anthology of people of yesteryear - arranged alphabetically by village or town.
JOHN BUNYAN: His Life and Times: Vivienne Evans. Highly praised and readable account.
THE RAILWAY AGE IN BEDFORDSHIRE: Fred Cockman. Classic, illustrated account of early railway history.
A LASTING IMPRESSION: Michael Dundrow. A boyhood evacuee recalls his years in the Chiltern village of Totternhoe near Dunstable.
GLEANINGS REVISITED: Nostalgic Thoughts of a Bedfordshire Farmer's Boy: E.W. O'Dell. His own sketches and early photographs adorn this lively account of rural Bedfordshire in days gone by.
BEDFORDSHIRE'S YESTERYEARS Vol 2: The Rural Scene: Brenda Fraser-Newstead. Vivid first-hand accounts of country life two or three generations ago.
BEDFORDSHIRE'S YESTERYEARS Vol 3: Craftsmen and Tradespeople: Brenda Fraser-Newstead. Fascinating recollections over several generations practising many vanishing crafts and trades.
BEDFORDSHIRE'S YESTERYEARS Vol 4: War Times and Civil Matters: Brenda Fraser-Newstead. Two World Wars, plus transport, law and order, etc.
DUNNO'S ORIGINALS: A facsimile of the rare pre-Victorian history of Dunstable and surrounding villages. New preface and glossary by John Buckledee, Editor of The Dunstable Gazette.

PROUD HERITAGE: A Brief History of Dunstable, 1000-2000AD: Vivienne Evans. Century by century account of the town's rich tradition and key events, many of national significance.
DUNSTABLE WITH THE PRIORY: 1100-1550: Vivienne Evans. Dramatic growth of Henry I's important new town around a major crossroads.
DUNSTABLE IN TRANSITION: 1550-1700: Vivienne Evans. Wealth of original material as the town evolves without the Priory.
OLD DUNSTABLE: Bill Twaddle. A new edition of this collection of early photographs.
BOURNE and BRED: A Dunstable Boyhood Between the Wars: Colin Bourne. An elegantly written, well illustrated book capturing the spirit of the town over fifty years ago.
OLD HOUGHTON: Pat Lovering. Pictorial record capturing the changing appearances of Houghton Regis over the past 100 years.
ROYAL HOUGHTON: Pat Lovering. Illustrated history of Houghton Regis from the earliest of times to the present.
GIRLS IN BLUE: Christine Turner. The activities of the famous Luton Girls Choir properly documented over its 41 year period from 1936 to 1977.
THE STOPSLEY BOOK: James Dyer. Definitive, detailed account of this historic area of Luton. 150 rare photographs.
THE STOPSLEY PICTURE BOOK: James Dyer. New material and photographs make an ideal companion to The Stopsley Book.
PUBS and PINTS: The Story of Luton's Public Houses and Breweries: Stuart Smith. The background to beer in the town, plus hundreds of photographs, old and new.
LUTON AT WAR - VOLUME ONE: As compiled by the Luton News in 1947, a well illustrated thematic account.
LUTON AT WAR - VOLUME TWO: Second part of the book compiled by The Luton News.
THE CHANGING FACE OF LUTON: An Illustrated History: Stephen Bunker, Robin Holgate and Marian Nichols. Luton's development from earliest times to the present busy industrial town. Illustrated in colour and mono.
WHERE THEY BURNT THE TOWN HALL DOWN: Luton, The First World War and the Peace Day Riots, July 1919: Dave Craddock. Detailed analysis of a notorious incident.
THE MEN WHO WORE STRAW HELMETS: Policing Luton, 1840-1974: Tom Madigan. Fine chronicled history, many rare photographs; author - served in Luton Police for fifty years.
BETWEEN THE HILLS: The Story of Lilley, a Chiltern Village: Roy Pinnock. A priceless piece of our heritage - the rural beauty remains but the customs and way of life described here have largely disappeared.
KENILWORTH SUNSET: A Luton Town Supporter's Journal: Tim Kingston. Frank and funny account of football's ups and downs.
A HATTER GOES MAD!: Kristina Howells. Luton Town footballers, officials and supporters talk to a female fan.

LEGACIES: Tales and Legends of Luton and the North Chilterns: Vic Lea. Mysteries and stories based on fact, including Luton Town Football Club. Many photographs.

THREADS OF TIME: Shela Porter. The life of a remarkable mother and businesswoman, spanning the entire century and based in Hitchin and (mainly) Bedford.

STICKS AND STONES: The Life and Times of a Journeyman Printer in Hertford, Dunstable, Cheltenham and Wolverton: Harry Edwards.

LEAFING THROUGH LITERATURE: Writers' Lives in Herts and Beds: David Carroll. Illustrated short biographies of many famous authors and their connections with these counties.

A PILGRIMAGE IN HERTFORDSHIRE: H.M. Alderman. Classic, between-the-wars tour round the county, embellished with line drawings.

THE VALE OF THE NIGHTINGALE: Molly Andrews. Several generations of a family, lived against a Harpenden backdrop.

SUGAR MICE AND STICKLEBACKS: Childhood Memories of a Hertfordshire Lad: Harry Edwards.Vivid evocation of gentle pre-war in an archetypal village, Hertingfordbury.

SWANS IN MY KITCHEN: Lis Dorer. Story of a Swan Sanctuary near Hemel Hempstead.

THE HILL OF THE MARTYR: An Architectural History of St.Albans Abbey: Eileen Roberts. Scholarly and readable chronological narrative history of Hertfordshire and Bedfordshire's famous cathedral. Fully illustrated with photographs and plans.

THE TALL HITCHIN INSPECTOR'S CASEBOOK: A Victorian Crime Novel Based on Fact: Edgar Newman. Worthies of the time encounter more archetypal villains.

SPECIALLY FOR CHILDREN

VILLA BELOW THE KNOLLS: A Story of Roman Britain: Michael Dundrow. An exciting adventure for young John in Totternhoe and Dunstable two thousand years ago.

THE RAVENS: One Boy Against the Might of Rome: James Dyer. On the Barton Hills and in the south-east of England as the men of the great fort of Ravensburgh (near Hexton) confront the invaders.

THE BOOK CASTLE, 12 Church Street, Dunstable,
Bedfordshire LU5 4RU
Tel: (01582) 605670 Fax (01582) 662431
Email: bc@book-castle.co.uk

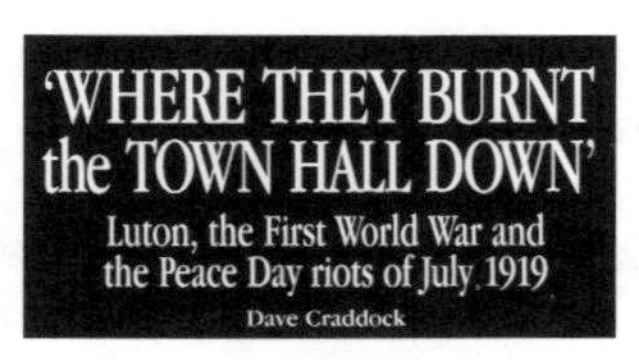

"WHERE THEY BURNT THE TOWN HALL DOWN"
Luton, The First World War and the Peace day Riots of July 1919

by Dave Craddock

The weekend of 19/20th July 1919 was arguably the most momentous in the history of Luton. What began as an afternoon of peace celebrations marking the end of the Great War turned into riots that had by the Sunday morning left the Town hall a smouldering, gutted ruin with the military in control of the town. Yet over the years, the story of the riots has been largely neglected. Drawing broadly on contemporary documents, witness statements and newspaper reports, the book gives a blow-by-blow account of the riots, their aftermath and subsequent trials. The hostility between the Town Council and ex-servicemen's organisations in the preceding months is also covered extensively, as is the impact of the First World War on Luton. Features of this book include informative appendices containing a wealth of information and over 50 illustrations.

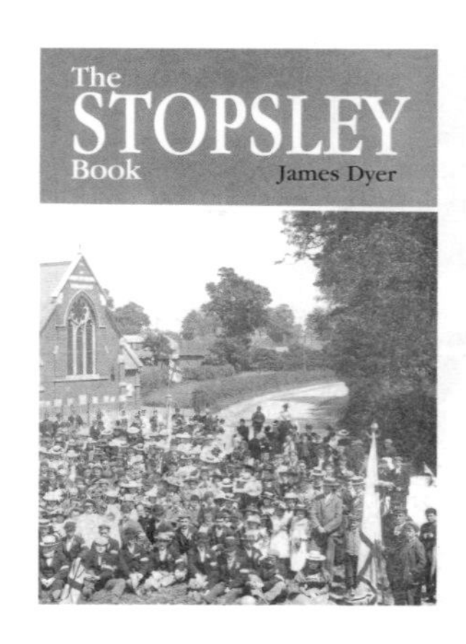

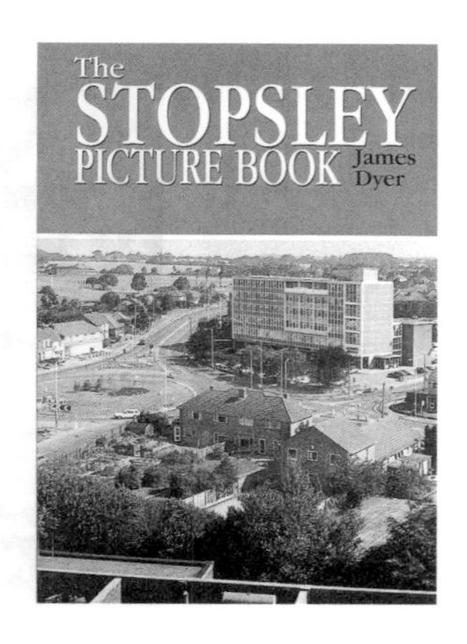

THE STOPSLEY BOOK
&
THE STOPSLEY PICTURE BOOK

by James Dyer

The hamlet of Stopsley, two miles from Luton in Bedfordshire, has a history that stretches back some 300,000 years. Situated in a region initially dependent on agriculture, straw plaiting and brick making, it can be seen as a microcosm of life in almost any village on the northern edge of the Chiltern Hills. The Stopsley Book tells the story of 20 farms, 16 schools and 4 churches within the civil parish which stretched from Someries Castle in the south to Galley Hill and the Icknield Way in the north. It looks in detail at almost every aspect of village life, particularly in the 19th and 20th centuries, and includes the work of the Parish Council, the weather, water and gas supplies, health care, policing, farm work, brick making and a wide variety of leisure pursuits. Based on thirty years of extensive search and interviews with local people, many now deceased; it is an exhaustive account of a community that still prides itself on its village spirit and individuality. It includes a collection of 146 photographs, many of which have not been published before. The Stopsley Book aroused such a great deal of interest in Britain and abroad that a number of readers submitted archive photographs of Stopsley and its surrounding area to the author. These are included in a The Stopsley Picture Book, which contains 150 photographs and carefully researched captions, to supplement the original work.